ENHANCING THE EMPLOYABILITY
OF DEAF PERSONS

ENHANCING THE EMPLOYABILITY OF DEAF PERSONS

—Model Interventions—

Edited by

STEVEN E. BOONE, PH.D.

and

GREGORY A. LONG, PH.D.

C H A R L E S C T H O M A S • P U B L I S H E R
Springfield • Illinois • U.S.A.

Published and Distributed Throughout the World by
CHARLES C THOMAS • PUBLISHER
2600 South First Street
Springfield, Illinois 62794-9265

© *1988 by* CHARLES C THOMAS • PUBLISHER
ISBN 0-398-05383-9
Library of Congress Catalog Card Number: 87-7127

Printed in the United States of America
Q-R-3

Library of Congress Cataloging in Publication Data
Enhancing the employability of deaf persons.

Includes bibliographies and index.
1. Deaf--Employment--United States--Case studies.
I. Boone, Steven E. II. Long, Gregory A. [DNLM:
1. Deafness--rehabilitation. 2. Employment.
3. Evaluation Studies. 4. Rehabilitation, Vocational.
HV 2551 E58]
HV2504.5.U6E53   1988   331.5'9   87-7127
ISBN 0-398-05383-9

CONTRIBUTORS

Glenn Anderson, Ph.D.

Arkansas Rehabilitation Research and Training Center
on Deafness and Hearing Impairment
Little Rock, Arkansas
Department of Rehabilitation Education
University of Arkansas
Fayetteville, Arkansas

Steven E. Boone, Ph.D.

Arkansas Rehabilitation Research and Training Center
on Deafness and Hearing Impairment
Little Rock, Arkansas
Department of Rehabilitation Education
University of Arkansas
Fayetteville, Arkansas

Michael Bullis, Ph.D.

Teaching Research Division
Oregon State System of Higher Education
Monmouth, Oregon

Gregory A. Long, Ph.D.

Arkansas Rehabilitation Research and Training Center
on Deafness and Hearing Impairment
Little Rock, Arkansas
Department of Rehabilitation Education
University of Arkansas
Fayetteville, Arkansas

Nancy M. Long, Ph.D.

*Arkansas Rehabilitation Research and Training Center
on Deafness and Hearing Impairment
Little Rock, Arkansas
Department of Rehabilitation Education
University of Arkansas
Fayetteville, Arkansas*

Paula Marut, M.A.

*Louisiana State School for the Deaf
Baton Rouge, Louisiana*

Douglas Watson, Ph.D.

*Arkansas Rehabilitation Research and Training Center
on Deafness and Hearing Impairment
Little Rock, Arkansas
Department of Rehabilitation Education
University of Arkansas
Fayetteville, Arkansas*

ACKNOWLEDGMENTS

I T IS WITH sincere appreciation that we acknowledge the many individuals and agencies that played a crucial role in the development of this book. Each of the individual chapter authors are to be commended for their efforts to conduct research projects directed toward enhancing the lives of deaf persons. In particular, we thank them for the clarity with which they shared information generated from their projects for this book.

Apart from the chapter authors, we owe a huge debt of gratitude to Ms. Sandra Pledger, who typed numerous drafts of the book manuscript, and to Ms. Brenda Broussard, who assisted in various aspects of the design of the book. Their efforts were invaluable.

Finally, we would like to thank the many agencies that allowed these interventions to be evaluated. Included among this list is the Arkansas School for the Deaf, the Southwest Center for the Hearing-Impaired, Arkansas Rehabilitation Services, Tulsa Speech and Hearing Association, Hot Springs Rehabilitation Center, and the Memphis, Tennessee School System.

This publication was made possible in part through research and training center grant number G008103980 — RT-31 from the National Institute on Disability and Rehabilitation Research (formerly the National Institute of Handicapped Research), United States Office of Education.

Steven E. Boone
Gregory A. Long

CONTENTS

ENHANCING THE EMPLOYABILITY
OF DEAF PERSONS

CHAPTER 1

EMPLOYABILITY ENHANCEMENT NEEDS OF DEAF PERSONS

STEVEN E. BOONE and GREGORY A. LONG

WORK, a highly valued activity in our society, occupies a significant portion of adult life. In addition to salary and the material
resources that it provides, employment meets a number of basic needs.
Work provides persons with the opportunity for social interaction, col-
lective purpose and regular activities over a structured time frame, as
well as personal status and identity (Jahoda, 1982). The meaning of
work and competitive employment is accentuated and especially important for the worker with a disability, going beyond wages and other
tangible benefits to represent an integral component of independence
and full integration into society (Crewe & Zola, 1983).

Despite the importance of work, it is unfortunate that the employment prospects for deaf individuals are less than optimal. Christiansen
(1982) reports that unemployment rates for hearing-impaired persons
have historically lagged behind the rates for the general population and
that unemployment is on the rise within the deaf population. Furthermore, other research (Vernon & Hyatt, 1981; Passmore, 1983) indicates
recent trends in employment show deaf people to be underemployed in
comparison to the general population. Recognizing these problems, a
large body of research in the last two decades has amassed descriptive
data regarding the employment status, achievements, problems, and
needs of deaf persons (Lunde & Bigman, 1959; Rainer, Altshuler, &
Kallman, 1963; Boatner, Stuckless, & Moores, 1964; Kronenberg &
Blake, 1966; Schein, 1968; Crammatte, 1968; Schein & Delk, 1974;
Passmore, 1983). Although these studies utilized varying methodologies

and often produced contradictory findings, they have repeatedly characterized the plight of the deaf worker as follows:

- Deaf workers are generally found in unskilled, semiskilled or otherwise manual occupations. There is very little representation of this population in professional and administrative occupations.
- These jobs are frequently characterized by low job security and little opportunity for advancement beyond entry-level.
- Many of these jobs pay low wages. Although reliable and stable employees, the average deaf worker earns only 72 percent as much as the average hearing worker in the labor force. Salaries of nonwhite deaf workers are even lower.
- Many of the occupations in which deaf workers are clustered are either declining in demand or projected to undergo only minimal growth. Advanced technology is rapidly replacing many of these occupations.
- Very few deaf workers are employed in rapidly increasing occupational clusters.
- Female and nonwhite deaf workers fare less well in obtaining employment. Although deaf males are employed at a rate comparable to, or slightly above, males in general, deaf females suffer 50 percent more unemployment than females in general. Nonwhite deaf persons do worse than nonwhite persons in general and far worse than white deaf males.
- Prevocationally deaf persons have greater difficulty obtaining employment. Their average educational attainment (years attended school) falls below that of the general population, further handicapping their ability to compete. Obstacles surrounding communication are important factors related to the earnings and occupational attainment of these workers.
- A significant proportion of deaf workers exhibit personal and/or work adjustment deficits of a magnitude to jeopardize their obtaining and/or retaining employment. Approximately 30 to 50 percent of the low-achieving rehabilitation client population present other disabilities in addition to deafness.

Responding to the stark realities presented by these research studies, the field of deafness rehabilitation has taken vigorous action on several fronts. Numerous comprehensive rehabilitation evaluation and adjustment training programs for multiply handicapped deaf clients have been funded (e.g., Lawrence & Vescovi, 1967; Blake, 1970; Hurwitz, 1971;

Berger, Holdt, & LaForge, 1972; Gellman, 1973; Watson, Bowe, & Anderson, 1973; Stewart, 1979). These programs have demonstrated various ways and means that some of the needs of this subgroup could be met through creative adaptations in personnel, techniques, procedures, curriculum, and related programming. Conclusions regarding the success of these efforts have been perhaps best articulated by Watson (1977):

> "Deaf persons have demonstrated the capacity to do almost any kind of work for which they qualify by virtue of education, abilities, and experience. No doubt some of the achievements attained by deaf persons are attributable to the considerable investments made by education and rehabilitation programs devoted to the career preparation of deaf persons" (p. 3).

As a result of these and related continuing efforts, there is now a much better understanding and appreciation of the service needs of this client group. However, despite these successes, it is important to note that unemployment and underemployment remain a significant problem for the deaf worker even following the provision of rehabilitation services. In an analysis of national R-300 data compiled by rehabilitation services, El-Khiami (1986) found that about 42 percent of deaf and 38 percent of hard-of-hearing persons receiving VR services in 1978 remained unemployed. Although much has been learned, there is much more to accomplish before the field can hope to better meet the needs of these individuals (Stewart, 1979; Ouellette & Lloyd, 1980; Schein, 1981). Programming is still needed to address the following areas:

- Few deaf workers have access to extensive and appropriate occupational information, counseling, and guidance in making career choices. The vocational aspirations and aptitudes of many indicate they have potential for higher level occupations than they normally obtain and/or hold.
- Many existing tests, vocational guidance services, adjustment training, skill training, job placement, and related techniques are grossly inadequate and too often unavailable to assist deaf clients in their vocational development. Few valid and standardized tools are on hand. Even fewer skilled counselors, evaluators, instructors, and psychologists are available.
- Few resources are available to assist in upgrading the skills of the underemployed, displaced, or otherwise terminated worker. Retraining and assistance in career mobility is virtually nonexistent.
- Although numerous research and development programs have been successful in serving some of the employment needs of deaf

persons, these programs have not yielded the hard, scientific research and development needed to produce the knowledge, tools, and techniques required to achieve real breakthroughs and advances.

A review of these statements leads to the conclusion that a need exists for a systematic program of research designed to develop and evaluate comprehensive employability enhancement services for this population. This need has been repeatedly recognized and articulated in a number of publications and national conferences by leaders in deafness rehabilitation since 1960 (Rogers & Quigley, 1960; Adler, 1970; Gough, 1977; Schein, 1981). In addition, these efforts should be based upon a comprehensive model of career development. All too frequently, efforts to enhance employment opportunities have focused on specific aspects of the placement process, with little attention to the integration of these activities into a continuum of career development. In many instances, rehabilitation and placement professionals have simply confused "employing" with "hiring" (Jamison, 1987). A series of integrated research activities addressing the full career development continuum is needed.

In response to the employability enhancement needs of deaf persons, the National Institute for Disability and Rehabilitation Research (NIDRR) established the University of Arkansas Rehabilitation Research and Training Center on Deafness and Hearing Impairment (RT-31). Following its mandate to investigate employability issues, RT-31 constructed a three-stage employability model to guide these efforts. As may be seen in Figure 1-1, this model is conceptualized as a funnel starting with a broad employability and life planning emphasis and ending with a focus on obtaining, maintaining, and advancing on the job. The first stage of the model, Life and Career Planning, focused upon the importance of goal-setting and the development of strategies to attain one's goals. This stage was considered crucial as numerous deaf rehabilitation clients are deficient in the knowledge required to establish and plan realistic goals for themselves, particularly with regard to employment. The second stage, Social and Job Preparation, emphasized the development of technical job skills as well as work-related social skills to appropriately conduct oneself during interactions with employers and co-workers. Deaf persons often have the vocational skills necessary for job success yet lack the necessary social skills to interact appropriately with others at the work place. Consequently, if these skills could be

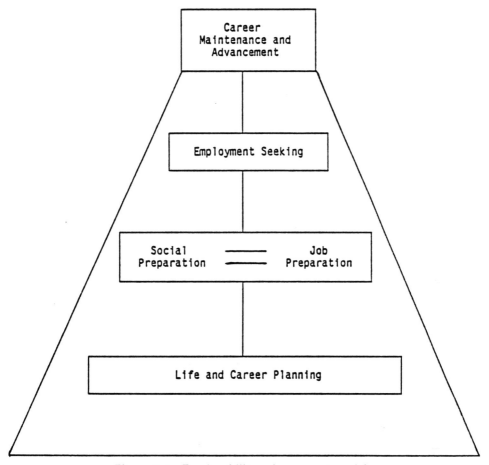

Figure 1-1. Employability enhancement model.

taught prior to the individual obtaining employment, the likelihood of maintaining employment would be greatly increased. The third stage of RT-31's employability model, Employment Seeking, centered upon the development of strategies and techniques for assisting deaf rehabilitation clients to explore occupational choices and actively prepare for seeking employment.

The purpose of this monograph is to describe the interventions associated with RT-31's employability model. The interventions are based upon research projects conducted during 1981-86. As such, each intervention has been field tested and evaluated regarding its effectiveness with deaf rehabilitation clients. Instead of focusing upon the technical aspects of these evaluations, each intervention will be presented in a chapter that includes a brief review of the literature regarding the intervention and its theoretical underpinnings, as well as a description of the ways the technique was modified for use with deaf persons. These discussions will be followed by a representative "case" example to illustrate the use of the technique with deaf clients. Thus, readers should gain an introduction to the range of interventions that may be used to enhance the employability of deaf persons as well as an overview of how to implement each intervention with their deaf clients. Readers interested in additional information regarding the research conducted to validate each intervention or information regarding the implementation of each intervention are urged to contact RT-31 or the individual authors of each chapter.

This monograph consists of eight chapters. Chapters Two and Three present interventions targeted toward Life and Career Planning; Chapter Four targets Social and Job Preparation; and Chapters Five and Six focus upon Employment-Seeking. In Chapter Two, Greg Long describes work on Goal-Setting Skills Training, a goal-setting and life-planning package that was designed for use with deaf persons. In Chapter Three, Mike Bullis overviews a typical model of career development and a method that targets teaching deaf individuals effective vocational decision-making skills. Moving into the Social and Job Preparation stage of the model, Chapter Four presents Nancy Long's use of Assertion Training with deaf adolescents and young adults. The third stage of the model, Employment-Seeking, is initially represented by an intervention developed by Paula Marut in Chapter Five. Within this chapter, Ms. Marut describes a computer-assisted Career Information Delivery System designed for use in occupational exploration with deaf persons. In Chapter Six, Nancy Long presents information on developing a Job Club for deaf persons.

In addition to discussing interventions associated with RT-31's Employability Model two supplimental chapters are included within this monograph. Chapter Seven presents information written by Steve Boone, Mike Bullis, and Glenn Anderson regarding ways to evaluate the effectiveness of various interventions using single subject research designs. These are an underutilized evaluation strategy that could enable rehabilitation professionals to hold their treatment methods responsible and accountable for enhancing the employability of their clients. In the final chapter, Douglas Watson and Glenn Anderson describe continuing employability needs of deaf persons and present an overview of a second generation of research designed to extend previous work conducted by RT-31 during 1981-1986.

REFERENCES

Adler, E. (Ed.). (1970). *Research trends in deafness: State of the art.* Washington, DC: Social and Rehabilitation Services.

Berger, D., Holdt, T., & LaForge, R. (Eds.). (1972). *Effective vocational guidance of the adult deaf.* Washington, DC: Rehabilitation Services Administration.

Blake, G. (1970). *An experiment in serving deaf adults in a comprehensive rehabilitation center.* (Final Report: RSA Grant R-1982). Hot Springs, AR: Rehabilitation Center.

Boatner, E.B., Stuckless, E.R., & Moores, D.F. (1964). *Occupational status of the young deaf adult of New England and the need and demand for a regional technical-vocational training center, Final Report.* West Hartford, CT: Vocational Rehabilitation Administration.

Christiansen, J.B. (1982). *The socioeconomic status of the deaf population: A review of the literature.* In J. Christiansen & J. Egelston-Dodd (Eds.), *Socioeconomic status of the deaf population* (Sociology of Deafness Monograph No. 4). Washington, DC: Gallaudet College.

Crammatte, A. (Ed.). (1968). *Multiply disabled deaf persons: A manual for rehabilitation counselors.* Washington, DC: Department of Health, Education, & Welfare.

Crewe, N., & Zola, I. (1983). *Independent living for physically disabled people.* San Francisco, CA: Jossey-Bass.

El-Khiami, A. (1986). Selected characteristics of hearing-impaired rehabilitants of general VR agencies: A socioeconomic profile. In D. Watson, G. Anderson, & M. Taff-Watson (Eds.), *Integrating human resources, technology, and systems in deafness.* Silver Spring, MD: American Deafness and Rehabilitation Association.

Gellman, W. (1973). *CJVS project for the deaf.* Final report SRS grant number 14-P-55171/5-OS. Chicago: Chicago Jewish Vocational Service.

Gough, J.A. (1977). *National training session on the rehabilitation of the deaf.* Las Cruces, NM: New Mexico State University.

Hurwitz, S.N. (1971). *Habilitation of deaf young adults* (Final report of SRS grant number RD-1804). St. Louis: Jewish Employment and Vocational Service.

Jacobsen, R., Vandergoot, D., Avellani, P., & Swirsky, J. (1978). *A review of placement services within a comprehensive rehabilitation framework.* Albertson, NY: Human Resources Center.

Jahoda, M. (1982). Employment and unemployment: A social psychological analysis. London: Cambridge University Press.

Jamison, S.L. (1987). Perspectives on Employment. In A.B. Crammatte (Ed.), *Meeting the challenge: Hearing-impaired professionals in the workplace,* (pp. 167-175). Washington, DC: Gallaudet University Press.

Kronenberg, H., & Blake, (1966). *Young deaf adults: An occupational survey.* Hot Springs, AR: Arkansas Rehabilitation Service.

Lawrence, C., & Vescovi, G. (1967). *Deaf adults in New England: An exploratory service program.* Final Report SRS-RD-1516-5. Boston: Morgan Memorial.

Lunde, A.S., & Bigman, S.K. (1959). *Occupational conditions among the deaf.* Washington, DC: Gallaudet.

Ouellette, S., & Lloyd, G. (Eds.). (1980). *Independent living skills for severely handicapped deaf people.* Silver Spring, MD: American Deafness and Rehabilitation Association, Research Monograph No. 5.

Passmore, D. (1983). Employment of deaf people. In D. Watson, G. Anderson, N. Ford, P. Marut, & S. Ouellette (Eds.), *Job placement of hearing-impaired persons: Research and practice.* Little Rock, AR: University of Arkansas Rehabilitation Research and Training Center on Deafness and Hearing Impairment.

Rainer, J.B., Altshuler, K.A., & Kallman, F.J. (Eds.). (1963). *Family and mental health problems in a deaf population.* New York: New York Psychiatric Institute, Columbia University Press.

Rogers, M., & Quigley, S. (1960). Research needs in the vocational rehabilitation of the deaf. *American Annals of the Deaf, 105*(4).

Schein, J.D. (1968). *The deaf community: Studies in the social psychology of deafness.* Washington, DC: Gallaudet College Press.

Schein, J. (Ed.). (1974). *Education and rehabilitation of deaf persons with other disabilities.* Silver Spring, MD: National Association of the Deaf.

Schein, J.D. (Ed.). (1981). *Model state plan for vocational rehabilitation of deaf clients: 2nd revision.* Silver Spring, MD: National Association of the Deaf.

Schein, J.D., & Delk, M.T. (1974). *The deaf population of the United States.* Silver Spring, MD: National Association of the Deaf.

Stewart, L. (1979). *Hearing-impaired developmentally disabled persons: A challenge to the helping professions.* Tucson, AZ: College of Education.

Vernon, M., & Hyatt, C. (1981). How rehabilitation can better serve deaf clients: The problems and some solutions. *Journal of Rehabilitation, 79,* 60-62.

Watson, D. (1977). *Deaf evaluation and adjustment feasibility.* Silver Spring, MD: National Association of the Deaf.

Watson, D., Bowe, F., & Anderson, G. (1973). Delivery of community services to deaf persons. *Journal of Rehabilitation of the Deaf, 14.*

CHAPTER 2

GOAL-SETTING SKILLS TRAINING FOR DEAF ADOLESCENTS AND YOUNG ADULTS

GREGORY A. LONG

THE ABILITY to establish goals and plan for their implementation has ramifications for numerous spheres of an individual's life. This is particularly true for employment and personal/social functioning as success in these spheres of living depends heavily upon the individual's ability to establish goals and act to carry them out. Hearing-impaired adolescents and young adults, however, may be at risk for the development of maladaptive goal setting skills. In a recent article, White (1982) identified several "areas of needed improvement" in hearing-impaired adolescents as reported by educators. Among the areas most urgently in need of improvement were an awareness of one's goals and developing the ability to make sound decisions.

There exists several hypotheses for explaining why hearing-impaired adolescents and young adults may be hindered in the development of their goal-setting skills. Language deficits may be involved in this situation. If adolescents or young adults do not possess the linguistic ability to express needs, desires, and feelings, then their behavior may likely be characterized by a high degree of impulsivity; a behavior that clearly mitigates against goal-setting and problem-solving skills (Harris, 1978). Meadow (1976) has additionally suggested that language deficits serve to limit the individual's ability to delay gratification and may therefore hinder efforts to teach a "work ethic" motivated by long term rewards. Language deficits have also been found to be related to rigidity. An individual with inadequate language development may learn and adopt one basic set of rules and strategies for dealing with the world that is then

11

utilized consistently without regard to the unique aspects of a particular situation. Another related explanation involves "psychocultural" or social learning deprivation, e.g., lack of exposure to the variety of input and feedback available to hearing adolescents within our culture and subsequent difficulties in goal-setting (Meadow, 1976).

DEVELOPMENT OF GSST

Goal-Setting Skills Training (GSST) was developed in response to these needs by researchers at the Arkansas Rehabilitation Research and Training Center on Deafness and Hearing Impairment. This package uses a systematic group counseling experience to facilitate individuals' abilities to establish goals for themselves and develop plans for their implementation. GSST was derived from Personal Achievement Skills training (PAS, Means & Roessler, 1976; Roessler & Means, 1976). The PAS program teaches goal-setting, communication, problem-solving, and behavioral self-control skills that can be used to augment psychosocial adjustment services in rehabilitation. Prior studies have documented the effectiveness of PAS in facilitating self-reported increases in goal-setting behavior and goal attainment with general rehabilitation clients (Roessler & DeWeese, 1975) and with visually handicapped persons (Roessler, 1978). In addition, Roessler, Cook, and Lillard (1976) found that PAS participants demonstrated gains in self-ratings of their life perspective, vocational and interpersonal maturity, vocational functioning, and goal attainment.

The development of Goal-Setting Skills Training involved several programmatic adaptations and modifications of the PAS components on goal-setting skills. The resulting GSST program included modifications in the language used, organization of the training into 10 specific curriculum activities, and changes in the assessment measures. In addition to simplifying the language used in the training materials, a number of examples were developed to highlight deafness-related issues in an effort to increase the intervention's realism and impact. The GSST program was divided into two major phases, goal definition and strategy development. The first five curriculum activities focused on goal definition and the second five focused on the behavioral specification of goals and program development for goal achievement.

Goal Definition

The first major phase of GSST, goal definition activities, is designed to facilitate group participants' awareness of the multitude of potential goals available to them in their daily lives (e.g., going to a movie, reading a book, obtaining a good job, going to college) and subsequent choice of a goal that is important to the participant. Emphasis is placed upon making goals as unambiguous as possible, based on the rationale that if goals are ambiguous, the plan of action to obtain the goal (i.e., program development activities) is doomed to failure. To ensure that goals are unambiguous they must be behaviorally and situationally defined with a stated time limit. For example, if an individual stated that he or she wanted to be "less critical" a problem arises as to the exact meaning of this goal. Where does the individual want to be "less critical." To whom? By when? This goal might be better stated as "To make four complimentary statements a day to my friends and family by October 9th."

Strategy Development

The second major phase of GSST, strategy development, is designed to help participants develop and select effective strategies to accomplish their goals. The essence of this phase involves identifying a behavioral goal and then specifying the performances required to reach that goal. After selecting a behavioral goal, the participant completes the remaining program development activities by: (a) specifying the steps, behaviors, or performance involved, (b) estimating deadlines for each step, and (c) projecting the anticipated results from each step.

Implementation of strategy development involves a six-step process. Initially, participants are taught that a program is similar to a game plan of things they will do to achieve a goal. Following this, the rules they should follow to develop a program and achieve their goals are:

Step 1: Behaviorally define the goal.
Step 2: Brainstorm ideas.
Step 3: Put the behaviors in steps from least to most difficult.
Step 4: Go back through the list of steps. Revise and refine the steps. Modify the steps so that each step is slightly more difficult than the previous step. Leave out any unnecessary steps. Make the last step your goal.
Step 5: Set a reasonable deadline for each step.
Step 6: State how many times you will practice each step.

Thus, Goal-Setting Skills Training proceeds through a sequential process wherein participants master the skills of goal definition prior to learning how to develop a plan of strategies for goal achievement.

GUIDELINES FOR IMPLEMENTATION

Setting

Goal-Setting Skills Training is not limited to any one particular setting. Although prior work with this package has been conducted within a group counseling setting, the basic components of the GSST program could also be conducted on a one-to-one basis. The physical setting for the group merely requires a location free of distractions, desks for the participants, and a blackboard. It is suggested that group meetings be conducted a minimum of twice a week for approximately 60 minutes. Approximately ten weeks are required to review and conduct each of the ten activities that compose the GSST curriculum. The actual time requirements for any one group, however, will vary as a function of the participants' interest and abilities.

Client Characteristics

Goal-Setting Skills Training is a group counseling technique that has wide applicability to a number of situations. Although the original model of Personal Achievement Skills training upon which GSST is based was designed to facilitate group participants' work adjustment skills, GSST is not limited to strictly work-related activities and/or situations. Rather, GSST is a generic strategy to help participants learn a conceptual model for behaviorally defining their goals and subsequently developing a structured, systematic series of steps for their attainment. As such, the range of appropriate problems and clients for which this method could be applied is almost unlimited.

There does appear to be at least one critical client characteristic that should be considered. In the research conducted with GSST, educational/intellectual skills appeared to be related to outcome. Applications of these materials appeared to be more successful for clients with higher intellectual skills as compared to groups who were intellectually average.

Service Provider Qualifications

To be an effective trainer with the GSST curriculum, the group leader should: possess a thorough knowledge of the training model, be enthusiastic, understand basic behavioral principles, and be able to establish trust and rapport with the participants. When conducting this curriculum with hearing-impaired participants, it is also essential that the group leader possess some fluency in the participants' primary mode of communication, most often that of manual communication. In addition, the group leader needs to be hyperalert to group processes and interactions. Since this is quite difficult for a solitary group leader, the use of a coleader is strongly encouraged.

APPLICATION OF GOAL-SETTING SKILLS TRAINING

To provide the reader with a brief introduction to the *process* of GSST, the following examples for each component of GSST are presented below. The first example illustrates goal development, which seeks to help participants understand what goals are, how to behaviorally define them, and how to establish goals for themselves. The second example illustrates the strategy development component of GSST, in which participants are instructed on how to brainstorm ideas, develop a hierarchy of steps toward their goals, and refine and revise their steps as necessary. These descriptions represent a "composite" interaction rather than a verbatim transcript of an actual session. The examples involve a leader (L) and eight group members (GM 1-GM 8).

Goal Definition

L:	Who can tell the group what we discussed last week?
GM 1:	We talk about different kinds goals.
L:	Right. Who can describe the three kinds of goals?
GM 2:	Daily detail goals. Like stuff do, no should do, but usually forget.
L:	Could you give me an example?
GM 2:	Like mow grass or polish car.
L:	Good. Could someone else tell me another type of goal?

GM 3:   Achievement goals. They take long time to finish. Like graduate high school.

GM 4:   And personality goals. They mean change something about myself.

L: Congratulations. You've remembered the three types of goals we discussed. Today, I want someone to volunteer one of their goals for us to discuss. Any volunteers?

GM 3:   I give one. I want to be more friendly.

L: OK. What do you mean "more friendly?"

GM 3:   I guess have more friends.

L: Good, that helps us understand what you mean better. Where do you want more friends? At school? In the dorm? When you're home with your family?

GM 3:   Mostly at school.

GM 2:   How soon you want new friends?

GM 3:   Today.

L: I'm sure you do but let's try to set a time so you can develop a plan for accomplishing your goal.

GM 3:   Maybe four weeks. That OK?

L: So your goal is to have more friends at school within four weeks.

As you can see, the leader has reviewed the previous week's activities and encouraged a student to share one of her goals. Note that the original goal, "to be more friendly," required some revision to meet the behavioral criteria of being situationally defined with a stated time limit for its completion. The next task is to take this goal and demonstrate how it would be developed within the program development phase of the GSST curriculum.

Strategy Development

L: Let's use Tina's goal "To have more friends at school," and brainstorm ideas about how she could make more friends. Feel free to give any suggestions. They can be things that are easy or difficult to do. Just remember, they should help Tina in developing a plan to accomplish her goal. I will write your suggestions on the blackboard as you give them to me.

GM 1:   She could smile more.

GM 4:   She could talk more in class.

GM 5:	Go to parties.
GM 6:	Ask for help with homework.
GM 7:	Become friends with cheerleaders.
GM 8:	Wear pretty clothes.
L:	Thank you. Those are all good suggestions. Tina, which one would be easiest for you to do? Which one would be hardest?
Tina:	I guess easiest smile more. Hardest . . . become friends with cheerleaders.
L:	All right. I'll write these on the board. Now, which of the other suggestions would be the easiest?
Tina:	Wear pretty clothes and then talk more in class.
L:	Good. You have two suggestions left. Which would be easier . . . to ask for help with your homework or to go to parties?
Tina:	Ask for help with homework.

Within this example the group leader emphasized brainstorming and had "Tina" rank order the steps generated by the brainstorming process. The next step in the brainstorming process would be to have Tina add any additional steps she felt were necessary and delete unnecessary steps. Finally, Tina would be asked to rank order the steps with the last step as her goal.

SUMMARY AND FUTURE DIRECTIONS

Goal-Setting Skills Training is a systematic group counseling package developed to facilitate hearing-impaired adolescents and young adults' abilities to establish goals for themselves and plan for their implementation. GSST is composed of ten activities divided into two general sections: Goal Definition and Strategy Development. Training proceeds in a sequential fashion wherein success with later activities depends upon mastery of previous activities.

The GSST curriculum, as previously stated, is most effective with those hearing-impaired individuals who function at the higher end of the continuum with respect to intelligence and language development. Individuals of average intellect and language skills may find the content too abstract and verbally laden. Such individuals, however, learn most effectively when instructional content includes both didactic/discussion material and action-oriented practice including role-playing, behavioral rehearsal, or in vivo practice. The combination of instructional strategies encourages an intellectual understanding as well as practice in performing the "learned" material. As such, the Goal-Setting Skills Training curriculum may well be effective across all individuals, regardless of intellect or language ability, with the addition of action-oriented practice to supplement didactic information.

As an additional positive contribution, the GSST curriculum encourages future planning. Participants are introduced to the concept that they can influence their future goals and activities by taking an active role in planning for their implementation. Detailed strategies are presented regarding how to best develop plans for attaining one's goals. Participants learn how to generate alternatives and rank-order them in terms of their difficulty. This strategy allows them to attain smaller goals in the process of obtaining their ultimate objective.

Future research with this package should address a number of questions. To what extent will the skills learned within the group generalize outside the training setting? What are additional participant characteristics that may influence the benefits derived from this technique? What are appropriate measures that might be better suited for assessing participants' growth following training? What are the long-term effects of the training? And, how might the addition of action-oriented practice add to the program's impact with lower functioning participants?

REFERENCES

Harris, R.I. (1978). The relationship of impulse control to parent hearing status, manual communication, and academic achievement in deaf children. *American Annals of the Deaf, 123,* 52-65.

Levine, E.S. (1963). Studies in psychological evaluation of the deaf. *Volta Review, 65,* 496-512.

Meadow, K.P. (1976). Personality and social development of deaf people. *Journal of Rehabilitation of the Deaf, 9,* 1-12.

Means, B., & Roessler, R. (1976). *Personal achievement skills: Leader's manual and participant's workbook.* Fayetteville, AR: Arkansas Rehabilitation Research and Training Center.

Roessler, R. (1978). An evaluation of Personal Achievement Skills training with the visually handicapped. *Rehabilitation Counseling Bulletin, 21*(4), 300-305.

Roessler, R., Cook, D., & Lillard, D. (1976). *The effects of systematic group counseling with work adjustment clients* (Research Report). Fayetteville, AR: Arkansas Rehabilitation Research and Training Center.

Roessler, R., & DeWeese, M. (1975). *Psychological education for high school students.* Unpublished manuscript, University of Arkansas.

Roessler, R., Hoffman, J., & Garber, T. (1980). *The contributions of Personal Achievement Skills (PAS) to work adjustment training: A replication and extension.* Unpublished research report. Fayetteville, AR: Arkansas Rehabilitation Research and Training Center.

Roessler, R., & Means, B. (1976). *Instructor's supplement: Program development and evaluation guidelines.* Fayetteville, AR: Arkansas Rehabilitation Research and Training Center.

Vernon, M. (1969). *Multiply handicapped deaf children: Medical, educational, and psychological considerations.* Washington, DC: Council for Exceptional Children.

White, K.R. (1982, Oct./Nov.). Defining and prioritizing the personal and social competencies needed by hearing-impaired students. *Volta Review,* 226-274.

CHAPTER 3

CAREER EDUCATION

MICHAEL BULLIS

THE PURPOSE of this chapter is to examine issues related to the career education of deaf students. Toward this end, the chapter consists of four sections. First, an introduction to career education is provided and an instructional technique for improving career planning/decision-making skills is described. Second, guidelines for implementing the intervention are offered. To elaborate on these guidelines a case example is provided in the third section. The manuscript concludes by identifying future directions for research and practice.

BACKGROUND

It is all too apparent that hearing-impaired persons, especially those with early profound deafness, experience multiple employment problems including high unemployment rates and massive underemployment. At least three categories of problems are responsible for this situation. First, in many instances problems are encountered because of the lack of a supportive service network in the community (e.g., independent living programs, minimal employment opportunities) (Sacks & Bullis, in press). Second, issues related to communication problems between workers who are hearing-impaired and their nonhearing-impaired employers and/or co-workers can contribute to unsuccessful placements (DiFrancesca & Hurwitz, 1969). Finally, in many cases individuals do not receive adequate training in school prior to entering the community.

In response to this last category of problems, the past 20 years have witnessed the emergence of a strong career education movement in schools and programs for deaf students (Dwyer, 1985; Ouellette & Dwyer, 1985). Essentially, the career education movement encompasses an educational philosophy that focuses on preparing the student to enter the community and represents a distinct shift from traditional academic instruction (e.g., English, history) to a more practical, functional emphasis. This preparation is broad in scope and includes vocational training (e.g., job placement, vocational skill development), development of independent living skills (e.g., money management, shopping), and instruction in social and leisure skills (e.g., interpersonal interactions, accessing a support network) (Brolin, 1978; Bullis, 1986; Halpern, 1985; Wilcox & Bellamy, 1982).

In the Fall of 1983, RT-31 began an investigation into the career education preparation of deaf adolescents. Given the breadth of knowledge in the field of career information, it was first necessary to establish a clear, specific objective for the project. This was accomplished through a review of the literature and a needs assessment. This process included the gathering of feedback from leading professionals in the area of career education with deaf adolescents (Bullis, 1985a, 1985b). This effort helped to identify:

1. The population of students most in need of career education services.
2. The program model (intervention strategy) that would be most appropriate for the prioritized group of students.
3. The content that should be emphasized in training.

The results indicated that project efforts should focus on high school students who are likely to either enter a community college program upon leaving the secondary grades, or to enter the community without a firm plan for work or living. Also, it was decided that the most appropriate intervention model should be a course that could be incorporated into a regular high school curricula. This course would emphasize career planning and decision-making skills.

THE STEP METHOD

A review of curriculum packages was conducted and the **Step Method: Learning and Practicing Thinking Skills** (DiFrancesca,

1978) was selected for use in this project. This training program is designed to teach students processes of critical thinking and how to apply these rules to practical situations, such as making career choices. The program's design and intent are logical, but no experimental study of its effectiveness has been conducted (DiFrancesca, 1983, personal communication). Consequently, the Step curriculum fit neatly into the content and research requirements of this investigation.

The Step training approach (DiFrancesca, 1978) was developed under the auspices of the California State Department of Education as a career education curriculum for deaf secondary students. The program is unique in that it was designed to teach critical thinking and decision-making skills within the vocational context. Some of the thinking skills that are taught include: goal-setting, achieving goals, and analyzing vocational problems. Further, it is structured to be success-oriented and individual in nature. For example, one exercise calls for students to examine and identify their vocational interests using a step-by-step approach. The approach is designed to be easily generalized to other exercises.

The curriculum, which is designed to be taught in groups of six to ten students, is composed of easy-to-follow instructions for the trainer and a variety of structured learning exercises for the student. Ideally, it is structured to be taught in two or three one-hour classes a week for a period of one academic year. There are three components in this curriculum: Part I — Thinking Skills I Use Now; Part II — Setting New Goals for Myself; and Part III — Planning for Career Goals. The exercises in Part I help the student to think in an organized and logical fashion. There are three stages in this unit: Helping students to realize that they are — or can be — successful in reaching goals; helping students to conceptualize individual goals; and developing the ability to identify behaviors that lead to success in achieving goals. In Part II, students apply their decision-making (DM) skills in establishing new goals and in constructing plans to reach these goals. Finally, in Part III students apply their thinking skills to establishing individual career goals and developing plans to attain these objectives. Since the content of each unit flows logically from the preceeding component, it is essential that the program sequence be followed.

Some initial research on the Step method with nonhearing-impaired students suggests that it is an effective strategy in teaching DM skills. For example, students involved in the training program showed a significant positive change in teacher ratings of their critical thinking behavior after completing the training program (DiFrancesca, 1980). In addition, a research project conducted under the aegis of the Department of Health, Education and Welfare (Johnson, 1977) to analyze career education materials ranked Step as the best vocational curriculum designed for use with deaf students.

GUIDELINES FOR IMPLEMENTATION

The following suggestions were drawn from the previous description of the Step Method and feedback from teachers who have used the package. These guidelines are categorized according to the conduct of training, client characteristics, and assessment issues.

Conducting the Training

- The trainer should be experienced in conducting training with small groups of persons.
- It is essential that the trainer become familiar with the Step package prior to implementing the instruction. The directions are described clearly and simply, but preparation is necessary to insure a smooth training process.
- Although it is possible to restructure the Step training to be conducted five times per week for one semester, the feedback that we have received suggests that this modification is not advisable. The teachers who have used the curriculum believe that the programs should be conducted over the course of the school year.
- It is crucial that the trainer has communication skills that are compatible with those of the students.
- Because so many of the exercises require students to develop plans specific to themselves, it is important that the trainer have a close personal knowledge of the student and the resources available in the community.

Client Characteristics

- The training appears most valuable for students in the latter years of high school who are beginning to prepare for exit into the community. However, the training could be used to improve thinking skills in more sophisticated younger students to help them plan their high school program.

- Step training seems applicable to students with a wide range of cognitive and communicative abilities.
- Although it is not mandatory, it seems to make sense to structure groups to be as homogeneous (e.g., age, handicapping condition) as possible. However, some mixing of the groups may be advantageous to provide diverse models for the students.
- A small group (8-10 persons) should be maintained.

Assessment Issues

- Assessment of decision-making skill is difficult to conduct and there are few measures designed to focus on this process. Consequently, it is recommended that multiple measures be used to evaluate the student's progress.
- Several published tests (e.g., Career Maturity Index) may be used to measure the subject's knowledge of the decision-making process.
- Perspectives of teachers and parents on the student's skill gains should be gathered in a structured fashion (e.g., rating scale).
- The homework that the student develops as part of the training should be monitored to gauge progress made in developing "real life" plans.
- There is some indication that training in critical thinking procedures will improve course grades (e.g., Greenberg, Kusche, Gustafson & Calderon, 1985); thus, attention should be paid to the student's overall academic profile.
- If possible, it would be valuable to follow the individual students' transitions into society to evaluate their success in community integration and the extent to which the plans are followed and helpful in facilitating community integration.

APPLICATION OF THE STEP METHOD

In order to clarify the decision-making model the following hypothetical illustration is offered. The example includes a review of how the Step model could be used with an individual student.

The Student

Lynn is an adolescent male who has been deaf since birth and has some residual hearing through amplification. He attended public elementary school until the seventh grade, but his parents were not pleased with the education that he received. Basically, he learned rudimentary academic skills through the aid of a part-time interpreter. Because so few deaf students were in the school, though, Lynn had little opportunity to learn and/or practice sign language.

Lynn was moved by his parents to the state residential school to begin eighth grade. It was a shock to Lynn to be around so many deaf persons, and he had difficulty understanding sign language, the principal form of communication used by the students. He was enrolled in classes to learn sign, however, and gradually picked up the skill and became able to communicate. As time went on though, he became dissatisfied with his education. He thought that school was boring, that he was not learning anything of substance, and that he could be happier and make more money elsewhere. At 16, after a lackluster academic career, Lynn dropped out of school.

The Problem

Upon leaving school Lynn tried unsuccessfully to find work. He told his parents that he wanted to make a lot of money, maybe become a movie producer or manage a night club. After eight months of sitting around the house and making minimal attempts to find a job, Lynn's father got him a job as a janitor at a local business. Lynn seemed to like the job and enjoyed being in the community. After several weeks, though, he began to complain of the low wages and the poor way he was treated by the other workers. He soon quit. At his parents' insistence he was able to secure another, similar janitorial job. Unfortunately, the same pattern was experienced: he did well for a short period of time, but then complained about the shortcomings of the job and quit. At the end of their rope, his parents took Lynn to a counselor who specialized in vocational counseling for deaf persons. At the referral they told the counselor that they felt that Lynn was lazy and didn't really want to work.

Analysis of the Problem

The counselor spent some time getting to know Lynn and learning of his predicament. It was the counselor's position that Lynn was not lazy, rather that he lacked critical thinking skills related to career planning and vocational decision-making. Specifically, the counselor thought that Lynn lacked the knowledge necessary to establish a clear and realistic career goal. His objective of being a movie producer or manager of a night club was not viable; nor was he able to generate an employment alternative to meet this goal. The alternative that his father offered, the janitorial job, was not consistent with his own career goal. And, even though he liked the job, he had difficulty adjusting to the work setting.

In line with Lynn's unrealistic career goals and his need to finish school, the counselor recommended that he re-enroll in high school where he could complete his education and be trained in a viable vocation. To guide his choice process the counselor recommended that Lynn be enrolled in a year-long class on career planning that utilized the Step curriculum.

Intervention

Lynn went back to school as a Junior. He was pleased to be around persons who signed and with whom he could communicate. He felt somewhat pressured to be in school but did enjoy the career planning class. The class consisted of nine students like Lynn, who were upper classmen and who were trying to figure out what they would do after leaving school. During the first part of the class the discussion centered on recognizing and thinking through problems. Lynn was surprised that there was a sequence of thought to follow prior to acting. Usually, he merely responded to a situation without thinking logically through the issues. He had never realized that he needed to specify what he wanted to accomplish — his goal — in such instances.

The initial exercises were difficult for Lynn and the others. Their class work required that they specify problems that they had encountered, to identify the goal they wanted to achieve in that situation, and ways they could achieve that goal. Many of the students had difficulty discriminating between a "good" goal and a "bad" goal. For instance, a problem that Lynn identified related to getting along with his father about his employment future. Lynn's immediate goal for the situation was to get his father to "shut up." The teacher worked with Lynn to show him that his goal was not desirable and helped him to alter the goal to emphasize getting along with his father and helping him to see that Lynn was, in fact, working to become employable. In line with this goal, Lynn worked on ways to talk to his father in a positive way and formulated responses he could make when talking with his father about the situation.

Later, the coursework began to focus on what kind of job each student wanted to secure after leaving school. Lynn stated that he definitely wanted to become a movie producer. The longer he examined this goal, however, the more he realized that it was an unrealistic objective. With the help of his teacher he began to reassess his career objectives. He began to look at what he wanted to get out of a job and what he was good at and liked to do. Lynn decided that since he like working around cars he wanted to set a career goal of mechanic. Review of the goal by Lynn and the teacher led to the conclusion that this was realistic and something that should be considered further.

Lynn then began to investigate how to become employed as a mechanic. This process mandated that he investigate training and employment options in the community. Through this investigation he identified four behavioral alternatives. The first alternative was to drop out of school and to search for a mechanic job. The second was to complete his last year of high school and to enroll in a one-year program in his senior year as a mechanic's helper, preparation that would enable him to secure a job at an entry level. The third alternative was to drop out of school and to enroll in a two-year mechanics program. The last option was to finish school and worry about employment later.

Lynn decided to reject the first and fourth alternatives. In considering both he decided that they would not help him reach his goal. After thinking for some time and talking with his parents, he decided to reject the third alternative as well. The option would not lead him to a high school diploma, and it was entirely possible that he might not like mechanics and might want to change vocations at some point. Without his high school diploma such flexibility would be extremely limited. Thus, the second alternative—completing school and the mechanic's helper program—seemed to make the most sense at this point in his life.

FUTURE DIRECTIONS

Career education of deaf students is critically important to their eventual community placement. Indeed, it is logical to believe that preparation to enter the "next environment" (i.e., the community) is a necessary part of secondary education. Further, it is clear that this emphasis should be broad-based and include vocational preparation, instruction in independent living skills, and training in social and leisure skills.

The project described in this chapter dealt with only a small part of the career education process: career planning and decision-making. Although this area is considered important for the student, much remains to be learned about this process. The following suggestions for future research are offered.

1. It is imperative that instruments be developed to measure decision-making skills reliably and accurately. Given that this process is crucial to adolescents, it is mandatory that viable ways to measure the process be established. Through such a measure we will be able to gauge a student's abilities, construct an intervention to remediate the deficiencies, and evaluate the true impact of the instruction.
2. The impact of the Step curriculum must be further investigated. The materials are practical, easy to use, and make sense. We do not, though, have a firm idea of their impact.
3. The investigations that are conducted on the decision-making process should not be bound by the measures that are used and the walls of the school. Precious little is known about the community integration of deaf adolescents and the ultimate effect training in critical thinking processes can have on that integration. It is mandatory that longitudinal studies be established with students involved in this type of intervention. It will only be through such close empirical inspection that we will gain a greater understanding of the decision-making process and its relevance for deaf students. Moreover, this type of approach is essential if we are to reduce and resolve the employment problems that beset this population.

REFERENCES

Brolin, D. (1978). *Life centered career education: A competency based approach.* Reston, VA: Council for Exceptional Children.

Bullis, M. (1985a). The nominal group technique: An approach for specifying career education objectives and priorities. *Journal of Rehabilitation of the Deaf, 18*(4), 6-13.

Bullis, M. (1985b). A dilemma: What and who to teach in career education programs. In M. Bullis & D. Watson (Eds.), *Career education for hearing-impaired persons: A review* (pp. 55-75). Little Rock, AR: Research and Training Center on Deafness.

Bullis, M. (1985c). Where do we go from here? In M. Bullis & D. Watson (Eds.), *Career education for hearing-impaired persons: A review* (pp. 97-112). Little Rock, AR: Research and Training Center on Deafness.

Bullis, M. (1986). *Conceptual model for the summer institute on secondary special education and transition: A starting point.* Salem, OR: Oregon Department of Education.

Crites, J. (1973). *Career maturity inventory.* Monterey, CA: CTB/McGraw-Hill.

DiFrancesca, S. (1978). *The step method: Learning and practicing thinking skills.* New York: The Psychological Corporation.

DiFrancesca, S. (1980). Developing thinking skills in career education. *The Volta Review, 80,* 351-354.

DiFrancesca, S. (1983, November). Personal communication.

DiFrancesca, S., & Hurwitz, S. (1969). Rehabilitation of the hard core deaf: Identification of an affective style. *Journal of Rehabilitation of the Deaf, 3,* 34-41.

Dwyer, C. (1985). Career education: A literature profile. In M. Bullis & D. Watson (Eds.), *Career education for hearing-impaired students: A review* (pp. 3-25). Little Rock, AR: Research and Training Center on Deafness.

Greenberg, M., Kusche, C., Gustafson, R., & Calderon, R. (1984). The PATHS Project: A model for the prevention of psychosocial difficulties in deaf children. In G. Anderson & D. Watson (Eds.), *The habilitation and rehabilitation of deaf adolescents* (pp. 243-262). Washington, DC: National Association on the Deaf.

Halpern, A. (1985). Transition: A look at the foundations. *Exceptional Children, 51,* 479-486.

Johnson, H.A. (1977). *A model prevocational program for hearing-impaired students in a public day class setting at the secondary school level.* Memphis, TN: Memphis Public Schools.

Ouellette, S., & Dwyer, C. (1985). A current profile of career education programs. In M. Bullis & D. Watson (Eds.), *Career education of hearing-impaired students: A review.* Little Rock, AR: Research and Training Center on Deafness.

Sacks, S., & Bullis, M. (in press). The training and employment of persons with sensory handicaps. In R. Gaylord-Ross (Ed.), *Vocational education for persons with special needs.* Palo Alto, CA: Mayfield Publishers.

Wilcox, B., & Bellamy, T. (1982). *Design of high school programs for severely handicapped students.* Baltimore: Paul Brookes.

CHAPTER 4

ASSERTIVENESS TRAINING WITH DEAF REHABILITATION CLIENTS

NANCY M. LONG

HISTORICALLY, literature addressing the "characteristic" personality styles of deaf people has pointed to the existence of a severe lag in social skills development concomitant with a significantly higher rate of behavior problems. The term "social skills," as used here, refers to any simple and/or complex interpersonal behaviors that contribute to an individual's effectiveness as part of a larger group (Argyris, 1965). In comparison with peer groups of nondeaf individuals, deaf persons of all ages have been described as emotionally and socially immature (Schlesinger & Meadow, 1972), and easily frustrated and lacking in insight and empathic ability (Rainer, Altshuler & Kallman, 1969). Although the deaf population does not exhibit a higher incidence of severe psychiatric disorders in comparison with the hearing population, it has been reported that deaf individuals display a greater incidence of behavior-based disorders characterized by impulsivity, short-sightness, and a paucity of internalized controls (Altshuler, 1972; Altshuler, Deming, Vollenweider, Rainer, & Fendler, 1976).

In a similar review of the literature on personality and adjustment of deaf persons, Bolton (1976) concluded that "many deaf adults are deficient in the common knowledge and basic social skills that the average hearing person takes for granted" (p. 9). These deficits in social skills may interfere with the establishment of healthy long-term work and personal relationships (Levine, 1956), and as such, could clearly serve to frustrate the vocational rehabilitation efforts undertaken by deaf clients. The need for training designed to assist deaf rehabilitation clients to enhance their social skills repertoire has been well documented (Ford, 1985). Such a social skills training program should focus on eradication of inappropriate social behaviors by replacing them with more appropriate behaviors.

One popular training technique used to remediate social skills deficits is assertiveness training. Originally pioneered by Salter (1949), Wolpe (1969), and Lazarus (1971), assertiveness training was developed with a dual focus: to assist individuals to overcome inhibitions in interpersonal situations (passive individuals) as well as to express themselves in ways that are not in violation of the rights of others (aggressive individuals). Alberti and Emmons (1974), authors of the most popular model for assertiveness training, defined the goal of assertiveness training in comprehensive terms. They identified the training product as "behavior which enables a person to act in his or her own best interests, stand up for himself (herself) without undue anxiety, to express his (her) feelings comfortably, or to exercise his (her) own rights without denying the rights of others" (p. 2).

Most assertiveness training programs currently being utilized in mental health and rehabilitation settings focus on behavioral dimensions including initiation, maintenance and termination of conversations; "standing up" for individual rights; initiation and refusal of requests; giving and receiving compliments; and recognition and expression of justified anger and annoyance in appropriate ways. Indeed, the scope of "assertiveness training" has broadened so much over the years that it may be more appropriately labelled as "comprehensive social skills training" (Bellack & Hersen, 1977).

Assertiveness/social skills training procedures have been successfully utilized with psychiatric populations (Goldstein, 1973; Hersen, Eisler, Miller, Johnson, & Pinkston, 1973), nonwhite adults (Cheek, 1977; Landau & Paulson, 1977), stutterers (Coleman, Butcher, & Carson, 1980), marital counseling clients (Eisler, Miller, Hersen, & Alford, 1974), job-seekers (Wheeler, 1977), and women experiencing difficulties in interpersonal and job-related situations (Coleman, et al., 1980). Success has also been reported for use of this technique in rehabilitation settings. Jung (1978) explained rehabilitation success in terms of the relevance this type of training may have for the disabled person in dealing with employment situations related to job-seeking (e.g., interviewing) and job-keeping (e.g., interacting with co-workers, preventing exploitation, and interacting appropriately with employers and supervisors subsequent to obtaining employment). While this literature points to the successful use of assertiveness training for the enhancement of socially skilled behavior, the use of assertiveness training as a social skills training technique with hearing-impaired persons has only begun to be systematically evaluated. To date, only two studies have documented the successful application of assertiveness training with hearing-impaired persons: servicemen who were originally hard-of-hearing (Sedge, 1982) and children under the age of 12 (Turnbow, 1983).

This chapter is derived from a project recently completed by RT-31 that studied the effects of assertiveness training on the social adjustment, self-image, emotional adjustment, aggressive/passive behaviors, and impulsivity of deaf rehabilitation clients. The results of the study offer encouragement for the utilization of the materials and guidelines developed for enhancing the assertive social skills of deaf clients. Perhaps the strongest recommendation for the program stems from the anecdotal information provided by the group leaders in the project. These people, counselors at a residential treatment facility for deaf adults, lauded the program for providing a systematic and structured means by which to address a topic that they had previously been addressing on their own instinct.

OVERVIEW OF "THE NEW ASSERTIVE YOU"

A review of the assertiveness training programs available resulted in the selection of two assertiveness training packages (Palmer, 1977; Alberti & Emmons, 1974) as a guide to develop "The New Assertive You" program. Activities included in the training program are designed to help participants to: (1) make accurate discriminations between aggressive, passive, and assertive behaviors; (2) identify, accept, and assert personal rights; (3) recognize and accept the rights of others; and (4) assert appropriate self-control in situations where communication difficulties are experienced. The range of topics addressed are reflected in the following Table of Contents derived from the participant's handbook. The training package consists of a Participant's Handbook and a Leader's Manual which are subsequently described.

```
Chapter 1  What is Assertive Behavior?
Chapter 2  Strength and Power and Making Choices
Chapter 3  Rights and Responsibilities
Chapter 4  Asking for What You Want
Chapter 5  Saying "No"
Chapter 6  How to Deal With Criticism
Chapter 7  How to Give and Accept Compliments
Chapter 8  Being the New Assertive You
```

Figure 4-1.

Participant's Handbook

The participant's handbook for "The New Assertive You" training package presents assertiveness/social skills concepts in a sequential fashion wherein information learned in previous chapters serves as a foundation for discussion of concepts presented in later chapters. Information is conveyed in simple terms and pictures are utilized when possible as an additional resource for explanation/discussion purposes. Although the vocabulary used in the assertiveness training program is likely to be abstract (e.g., assertive, aggressive, passive), understanding the terminology is an important step to incorporate social skills into a person's repertoire. The following excerpt illustrates the initial description of the aggressive person as depicted in the participant's handbook. The participant's handbook was written keeping in mind the below average reading level reported for deaf people (3rd-4th grade; Trybus & Karchmer, 1977).

Some people ask for what they want by stomping, yelling, grabbing, pushing and pulling. They get what they want by being mean to other people and by hurting them. These people are called aggressive and they do not know how to get along with other people.

How can you spot an aggressive person? What does an aggressive person look like?

Figure 4-2.

Where appropriate, space was set aside for participants to respond to questions posed as part of a chapter topic (e.g., list personal strengths).

Leader's Manual

The strength of any training program lies squarely on the shoulders of the group leader. "The New Assertive You" leader's manual was developed to provide thorough guidance to leaders utilizing this assertiveness training program. Each chapter of the leader's manual is divided into five parts including: session objectives, introduction and rationale, participant's manual chapter, exercises, and carry-over assignments. These sections include suggested scripts of ways to introduce concepts and to encourage appropriate group responses.

GUIDELINES FOR IMPLEMENTATION

Setting

Implementation of "The New Assertive You" requires a group setting for optimal results due to its reliance on peer interaction and feedback. Physical surroundings should be conducive to a focused group meeting, i.e., free of distractions and comfortable. Group size should be kept to a comfortably managed size depending on communication mode and language skills of group members. Usually, groups with coleaders should be no larger than 10 persons.

The assertiveness training package was designed to have participants meet twice a week for one and one-half hours per session. Based on this schedule it will take approximately two months to complete the curriculum. However, it is recommended that this time guideline be considered as a minimum. Groups of less skilled, lower functioning clients may require daily meetings of one hour or more for a longer duration to successfully complete the curriculum.

Client Characteristics

The "New Assertive You" program is designed for deaf persons with approximately a third-grade reading level. Persons likely to benefit from this type of training are those for whom employment and social possibilities are limited due to utilization of inappropriate social skills. It is imperative that group composition be based on two factors: clients' pretraining assertiveness capabilities and commonality of communication mode. Regarding assertiveness capabilities, group leaders should strive to obtain a mixture of clients, i.e., both overly passive and aggressive individuals. It is recommended, however, that discretion be used regarding the inclusion of too many highly aggressive group members as these individuals may tend to dominate and/or intimidate the more passive group members. Commonality of communication mode is also an important consideration as group members will obtain training benefits most readily when communication barriers are kept to a minimum.

Service Provider Qualifications

Effective group leaders of assertiveness training with deaf clients must have a thorough knowledge and understanding of the training model and training package being utilized. These trainers should also possess fluency in the primary mode of communication of the group members; most often this requires fluency with ASL and the ability to communicate effectively with persons who have minimal language skills. It is further strongly recommended that groups be led by teams of two coleaders.

APPLICATION OF "THE NEW ASSERTIVE YOU" PROGRAM

To illustrate the use of these materials, the following example was derived from the suggested scripts in the leader's manual and "typical" participant responses. The content for the example relates to the material in the participant's handbook previously described, and is designed to introduce participants to the concepts of assertive, aggressive, and passive behavior. The materials emphasize the physical components associated with assertive behavior. The examples involve a leader (L) and six group members (GM 1-GM 6).

L: Now that you've read your handbook, let's discuss the idea of assertive behavior. Assertive is a new word. To be assertive means standing up for your rights without hurting other people. But, it means more than just that. Being assertive means being honest. An assertive person tells his ideas, thoughts, and opinions and at the same time does it in a way that shows respect for the rights and feelings of other people. What does assertive mean?

GM 1:	Be honest. Show respect to others.
L:	That's right. When do you show respect?
GM 2:	When talk others about rights.
L:	Right. What does an assertive person look like? He stands up tall and straight, looks directly at the person he is talking with and does not push or shove or shout.
GM 3:	Assertive person doesn't push?
L:	Right. An aggressive person is pushy and rough and doesn't think about other peoples' feelings or rights. An aggressive person makes others feel bad.
GM 2:	I feel bad when others pushy to me. Hurts my feelings.
L:	Yes, most of us don't like pushy people. They make us feel bad.
GM 4:	Suppose I ignore other people feelings. That aggressive?
L:	Yes it is.
GM 4:	Sometimes I need tell people stuff. If not, take advantage of me.
L:	I understand. Sometimes if you let others run over you, you feel bad because you don't get to tell them how you feel. That's called passive behavior.
GM 5:	What mean passive?
L:	Passive behavior means that you do **not** stand up for your rights and feelings. Understand?
GM 5:	Yes.
L:	Let's practice assertiveness. (Leader models an assertive pose.) How do I look now?
GM 6:	Stand straight and look right at me.
L:	That's right. What kind of behavior do you call that?
GM 2:	Assertive behavior.
L:	OK. (Leader models passive behavior.) How do I look now?
GM 4:	Shy, afraid.
L:	What do you see that makes me look shy and afraid?
GM 1:	Looking down.
GM 3:	Shoulders dropped.
GM 4:	Sad face.
L:	That's right. OK, how could I try to look assertive — strong?
GM 5:	Stand straight and look up.

This process continues until clients can readily identify and distinguish between assertive, passive, and aggressive behavior. Participants also practice being assertive in response to various situational examples posed by the leader.

L: Suppose, a man is standing in line to buy cigarettes. Another man pushes him out of line and takes his place. How is the second man acting?

GM 3:   Aggressive.

L: How does the man pushed out of line feel?

GM 5:   Mad or embarrassed.

L: What should the man do to be assertive?

GM 1:   Stand tall, look at man and say "That was my place in line."

L: OK, let's practice doing that. Bill, will you show me how you should act in that situation?

GM 2:   OK. (Participants role-play the situation and the leader requests and provides feedback regarding their performance.)

L: Good. How did Bill look?

GM 1:   Assertive. He stood tall.

GM 2:   Strong.

L: Let's practice another situation.

This process continues with the leader shaping participants' descriptions and physical behavior until each can identify and act out the physical components of assertive behavior. Homework assignments are used to help participants facilitate the use of the skills they are learning in their lives. For example, participants might be instructed to keep an "assertiveness diary" after the lessons. This diary will be the basis for future carry-over assignments and will serve to aid the participants in making the transition to using the skills learned in the sessions to everyday situations outside of session meetings. For example, the carry-over assignment for the aforementioned group meeting might be to note situations where people are not acting assertively and how they might alter their behavior to be more appropriately assertive.

SUMMARY AND FUTURE DIRECTIONS

"The New Assertive You" is a training program designed to facilitate the development of appropriate social skills by deaf adults whose inappropriate social skills cause difficulties in employment and other interpersonal situations.

It is recommended that future directions with this training program revolve around the selection or modification of assessment instruments that will accurately assess and be sensitive to changes in the assertive/ social skills of deaf persons, a need underscored in the evaluation of this project. In addition, it is recommended that efforts be undertaken to expand on the basic concepts presented in this intervention strategy. Specifically, efforts should be addressed to "build" upon the concepts presented in these assertiveness training materials and then focus on the remediation of specific deficits exhibited by clients. Thus, these endeavors would best be tailored to individual client needs, with reference back to the basic concepts learned (e.g., responsibilities, others' rights). This type of comprehensive approach combining abstract discussion of assertion principles with practice and learning ways to behave more assertively would likely serve to more effectively enhance the appropriate social skills of many deaf clients.

REFERENCES

Alberti, R.E., & Emmons, M.L. (1974). *Your perfect right.* San Luis Obispo, CA: Impact Publishers.

Altshuler, K.Z. (1972). Reaction to and management of sensory loss: Blindness and deafness. In B. Schoenberg (Ed.), *Loss and grief: Psychological management in medical practice,* (pp. 140-155). New York: Columbia University Press.

Altshuler, K.Z., Deming, W.E., Vollenweider, J., Rainer, J.D., & Fendler, R. (1976). Impulsivity and profound early deafness: a crosscultural inquiry. *American Annals of the Deaf, 121,* 331-345.

Argyris, C. (1965). Explorations in interpersonal competence – I. *Journal of Applied Behavioral Science, 1,* 58-83.

Bellack, A.S., & Hersen, M. (1977). *Behavior modification: An introductory handbook.* Baltimore, MD: The Williams & Wilkins Company.

Bolton, B. (Ed.). (1976). *Psychology of deafness for rehabilitation counselors.* Baltimore, MD: University Park Press.

Cheek, D.K. (1977). Assertive behavior and black lifestyles. In R. Alberti (Ed.), *Assertiveness: Innovations, applications, issues.* San Luis Obispo, CA: Impact Publishers.

Coleman, J., Butcher, J., & Carson, R. (1980). *Abnormal psychology and modern life,* Glenview, IL: Scott, Foresman and Company.

Eisler, R., Miller, P.M., Hersen, M., & Alford, H. (1974). Effects of assertive training on marital interaction. *Archives of General Psychiatry, 30,* 643-649.

Ford, N.M. (1985). Assertiveness training as a behavioral intervention with deaf persons. In D. Watson & B. Heller (Eds.), *Mental health and deafness: Strategic perspectives.* Silver Spring, MD: American Deafness and Rehabilitation Association.

Goldstein, A.P. (1973). *Structural learning therapy: Toward a psychotherapy for the deaf.* New York: Academic Press.

Hersen, M., Eisler, P.M., Miller, P.M., Johnson, M.B., Pinkston, S.G. (1973). Effects of practice, instructions, and modeling on components of assertive behavior. *Behavior Research and Therapy, 11,* 443-451.

Jung, H.F. (1978). Assertiveness training: A new tool for rehabilitation. *Psychosocial Rehabilitation Journal, 2,* 24-29.

Landau, P., & Paulson, T. (1977). Group assertion training for Spanish Mexican-American mothers. In R. Alberti (Ed.), *Assertiveness: Innovations, applications, issues.* San Luis Obispo, CA: Impact Publishers.

Lazarus, A.A. (1971). *Behavior therapy and beyond.* New York: McGraw Hill.

Levine, E.S. (1956). *Youth in a soundless world: A search for personality.* New York: New York University Press.

Palmer, P. (1977). *The mouse, the monster and me!* San Luis Obispo, CA: Impact Publishers.

Rainer, J.D., Altshuler, K.Z., & Kallman, F.J. (Eds.). (1969). *Family and mental health problems in a deaf population* (2nd ed.). Springfield, IL: Charles C Thomas.

Salter, A. (1949). *Conditioned reflex therapy.* New York: Capricorn, Inc.

Schlesinger, H.S., & Meadow, K.P. (1972). *Sound and sign: Childhood deafness and mental health.* Berkeley, CA: University of California Press.

Sedge, S.K. (1982). Assertiveness training with hearing-impaired persons. *Rehabilitation Counseling Bulletin, 25,* 146-152.

Trybus, R.J., & Karchmer, M.A. (1977). School achievement scores of hearing-impaired children: National data on achievement status and growth patterns. *American Annals of the Deaf, 122,* 62-69.

Turnbow, K. (1983). *The effects of assertiveness training on exploratory assertive behaviors, sociometric status, and self-concept in the deaf.* Unpublished doctoral dissertation, University of Arkansas, Fayetteville.

Wheeler, K. (1977). Assertiveness and the job hunt. In R. Alberti (Ed.), *Assertiveness: Innovations, applications, issues.* San Luis Obispo, CA: Impact Publishers.

Wolpe, J. (1969). *The practice of behavior therapy.* New York: Pergamon Press.

CHAPTER 5

THE USE OF CAREER INFORMATION DELIVERY SYSTEMS IN THE EMPLOYABILITY SKILLS ACQUISITION OF DEAF PERSONS

PAULA MARUT

MANY DEAF workers, especially those with additional disabling conditions, are in a limited number of unskilled and semiskilled occupations characterized by low wages, poor job security, and little opportunity for advancement. Many of these jobs are rapidly becoming obsolete due to technological advances; others fail to harness the full vocational potential of the deaf worker and thus, lead to the problem of underemployment (Passmore, 1983).

As a rationale for these problems, various authors note that many deaf persons are not exposed to the wide range of vocational opportunities available in the labor market and thus, base their career choice upon consideration of an **inadequate, limited** range of occupations in which deaf persons have been traditionally employed (Austin, 1974; Fitch, 1976; Watson, 1976; Schein, 1977; Watson, Anderson, Marut, Ouellette, & Ford, 1983). To remediate this problem, one would assume that these persons could benefit from assistance directed toward career information, planning, and selection. Interventions need to be designed to provide deaf persons the relevant information necessary to make appropriate career choices from a larger selection of occupations. This need was underscored in a recent survey of career education programs conducted by RT-31 that identified career choice and planning as the most serious obstacle for deaf students preparing to enter the labor market (Bullis & Watson, 1985).

Conducted as an initial step in the development of career-oriented interventions, a literature review identified the availability of a computer-assisted Career Information Delivery System (CIDS) as the preferred strategy for general use. Developed by the National Occupational Information Coordinating Committee (NOICC) in response to federal mandates, these systems are available in all 50 states and are designed to provide an easily accessed body of occupational information as well as a description of the labor market in each state. Each CIDS system shares a common set of basic objectives:

1. Help students and clients learn about and understand the range of career opportunities presently available and those that are likely to be available in the future;

2. Help entrants to the labor force become aware of occupations they would find acceptable and personally satisfying;

3. Encourage persons in the process of career exploration and decision-making to seek out vocational information on their own;

4. Increase awareness of major sources of occupational, educational, and training information;

5. Help people learn of educational and training opportunities and their relationship to occupations they may be exploring;

6. Provide support for related programs including career education, career and employment counseling, employment training, and educational planning (Dunn, 1982).

The statewide Career Information Delivery System (CIDS) provides comprehensive national, state, and local information to individuals who are in the process of occupational exploration and/or a job search. By October, 1984, there were 13,406 institutional user sites in operation throughout the United States and its territories, including educational institutions, employment security offices, employment and training centers, vocational rehabilitation agencies, libraries, and business and industry. The variety of user sites assures reasonably easy access to this system by the general public. The use of computer assisted technology has significantly enhanced individuals' ability to access vast amounts of vocationally-related information quickly and efficiently. Despite these general advantages, it was determined that without modification, the utilization of this technology is limited for hearing-impaired persons.

ADAPTATION OF CIDS FOR
HEARING-IMPAIRED PERSONS

The specific software package to be described was jointly developed by the State Occupational Information Coordinating Committees in Maine and Michigan and is being implemented in several states currently using microcomputers for occupational information delivery. At present, the adapted system is designed for use on Apple II series computers. The CIDS adapted for hearing-impaired persons includes a list of 386 occupational titles and related descriptive information specific to the Arkansas labor market where the project was conducted. This system breaks the search process into two distinct components: (1) **The Self-Directed Search** which is designed to assist individuals to generate a list of occupational titles that match their interests; and (2) **Occupational Exploration and Information Gathering** which is designed to provide individuals with a variety of information relevant to a specific job. These components were developed to work together but could be used separately if so desired.

Self-Directed Search. The Self-Directed Search is designed to aid the individual in identifying interests and career goals via seven routes (or questions) that require persons to make specific decisions or choices. The seven choices comprise the individual's interest profile that leads to the generation of a list of occupational titles. This list of titles may be explored with the goal of narrowing the list and developing a career plan.

The search process is straightforward, simply requiring users to read, understand the computer-generated prompts, and subsequently make choices regarding their interests. For persons capable of these tasks, the package is self-administering. However, for other persons, it may be necessary to provide assistance in using the system depending upon the communication skills and experiential level of the hearing-impaired user. This assistance may include, but is not necessarily limited to, (1) adapting wording to the language skill of the user, and (2) instructing the user in the operation of a microcomputer.

Occupational Exploration and Information Gathering. Upon completion of the search, the user reviews the occupations generated, selects those they desire to further explore and begins the second phase of the package. Information regarding occupations is stored on microfiche cards that include eleven distinct files of information. The three major files of greatest utility for use with deaf persons include:

1. **The Occupational Index:** This file describes 386 general occupational categories and lists over 1,450 specific jobs. A variety of information is included for each occupation specifying the nature of the occupation, its corresponding duties and occupational specialties, tools used in the trade and working conditions, worker requirements and training needed, opportunities for experience in the occupation, methods to enter, earnings, advancement opportunities, benefits, typical career ladders, and employment outlook in each state. Related occupational categories are discussed and a set of review questions to check understanding of the material is included.

2. **National Postsecondary Schools Offering Services to Hearing-Impaired Students Index:** This file contains 62 schools with current enrollments of 15 or more students with hearing impairments and an organized support system in place to meet their needs. Information presented for each school includes a general description of the school and its location, requirements for admission and preparatory activities, special services available, costs, and programs offered.

3. **National Rehabilitation Facilities Offering Vocational Trade Training to Hearing-Impaired Persons Index:** This file lists 45 rehabilitation facilities that offer vocational trade training, accept out-of-state referrals, and offer specialized programming for hearing-impaired persons. Information includes a general description of the program, admission requirements, special services available, costs, and the specific vocational training programs that are offered.

A number of other files are included in the microfiche. These files, which may be less useful in work with hearing-impaired persons, include indexes of training programs available to the general public in the state of Arkansas:

4. **Postsecondary Program Index**
5. **Postsecondary School Index**
6. **Postsecondary Financial Aid Index**
7. **School Subject Index**
8. **Military Training Opportunities Index**
9. **Military Officer Training Index**

10. **Adult Education Programs Index**
11. **Arkansas Mentor Directory Index**

Modifications Required. As indicated in the introduction, a number of modifications were made to improve the accessibility of the original CIDS package to persons with severe hearing impairments. Initially, it was necessary to change the reading level required to utilize these materials. Many hearing-impaired persons possess substandard reading skills; reading achievement, especially that of prelingually deaf persons, is on the average equivalent to a fourth-grade reading level (Gentile, 1972; Furth, 1973; Moores, 1982). Unfortunately the majority of printed materials written for the general public is on a sixth-grade reading level. Thus, in order to make CIDS materials accessible, it was necessary to lower the language level. A related modification in the CIDS materials involved increasing the amount of information in order to enhance the user's understanding of the search process. These modifications included increasing the number of intermediate steps in the questions used in the search process. Care was taken to avoid vocabulary and sentence structures that were difficult to understand.

A second major modification involved one of the routes used in the search. When using the physical capabilities route, persons are asked if they want work that requires them to "talk and hear" on the job. If clients answer no to this question, a number of job titles are deleted from the options generated in the search. Unfortunately, many deaf persons interpret this question in relation to their sensory deficits. To remedy this problem, a modification of the software resulted in the addition of 143 occupations that were originally deleted from the options generated by answering this question "no." The jobs that were added to the search were derived from RSA R-300 data as jobs in which deaf persons were successfully placed during 1981.

A third major modification involved the creation and addition of two microfiche files that provide training information specific to the unique needs of deaf persons, the National Postsecondary Schools Offering Services to Hearing-Impaired Students Index and the National Rehabilitation Facilities Offering Vocational Trade Training to Hearing-Impaired Persons Index. Both of these files provide information regarding training opportunities and support services available to deaf and hearing-impaired persons on a national basis.

GUIDELINES FOR IMPLEMENTATION

Setting

The Career Information Delivery System was conceived to provide occupational information to persons across a wide variety of ages and backgrounds. As such, CIDS has application virtually anywhere that the issue of occupational exploration or employment is appropriate. With deaf persons, its use would parallel that of the general population. Specific suggestions for use would include but not necessarily be limited to:

The vocational evaluation. The search process can be incorporated in place of or in addition to a vocational interest inventory. The resulting occupational information can then be utilized as part of the exploration process and augment the work sampling.

Career counseling or career education training. The occupational information can provide up-to-date input regarding jobs under consideration, especially information specific to the local labor market.

Placement efforts. Job titles generated by the search process may provide additional occupations not already under consideration. Labor market information included in the package provides easily accessed projections regarding the advisability of pursuing specific job choices.

Prevocational educational settings. This would provide students exposure to the realities of the world of work. Teachers could utilize the package to develop the vocabulary and concepts necessary to deal with occupational issues. Decision-making skills could be applied to the search process as well as to determining which occupations to pursue. (See Chapter 2 for a more detailed discussion of career decision-making).

Client Characteristics

Individuals who would be appropriate users of this system would share some, but not necessarily all, of the following characteristics:

1. Some degree of interest in exploring the world of work.
2. Interest in entering the work force.
3. Contemplating a career change.
4. Participating in a vocational evaluation.
5. Participating in a career exploration/education class.

There are no set guidelines regarding age, though the junior high school level is generally when students are introduced to the idea of the world of work and careers (Bullis, 1985). The modified CIDS package is most appropriate for those users with hearing impairments sufficient to interfere with their ability to communicate with the hearing population through the use of speech and residual hearing.

The primary prerequisites to using CIDS are an interest in entering the job market or making a job/career change. The reading comprehension level of the individual will, however, affect the amount of assistance required on the part of the helping professional. For example, the user will need a minimum of a sixth-grade reading level to be able to complete the search process without assistance. In addition, data from the pilot evaluation of the CIDS package revealed that the higher the individual's reading comprehension the more inclined the user was to explore occupations that were: (a) unfamiliar and (b) different from those in which he or she had received vocational training. Regardless of the academic skills of the hearing-impaired users, however, the system is accessible if a professional capable of meeting their communication needs is available to explain the search process and occupational information gathering process.

Service Providers

As alluded to in the previous section, communication is a primary issue with this population. CIDS has been developed with self-administration as the goal. Because of the common problem of reading difficulties on the part of the hearing-impaired user, however, the professional must be able to accurately and impartially communicate the written CIDS information in order to facilitate its use.

Traditionally, service providers involved with this kind of package have included Vocational Evaluators, Placement Specialists, Career Education Instructors, Vocational Rehabilitation Counselors, and related personnel. With a deaf population, the ability to communicate using their language modality is generally the most important additional skill necessary. Many deaf persons converse via some form of manual communication. Therefore, competency in manual communication or the use of a qualified interpreter may be necessary to convey written information to these individuals.

APPLICATION OF CIDS

An illustration of the use of CIDS is provided in the following example. This example depicts use of the system with a person who has good reading skills and who completed the search independently. As previously discussed, some clients may require more assistance by the evaluator in answering questions and defining terms during the search process. Following a brief description of the information used to introduce and prepare the searcher, information included in boxes illustrates the actual material that would be seen on the computer screen.

The evaluator should cover and explain the following information prior to starting the search process:

- This is not a test—there are no right or wrong answers. Only answers that are right for you.
- You will be using a book that will ask you seven questions about yourself.
- The book may remind you of a test but it is not. It will ask you seven questions about things that you do and do not want to do.
- After you have finished answering the seven questions you will "enter" your answers into the computer.
- The computer will "read" your answers and print a list of jobs you should enjoy doing.
- It is very important that your answers are true about yourself **or** the computer cannot provide a good list of jobs for you.
- It is important that you ask me when you don't understand questions because you may give an answer that is not your true opinion.
- After your computer prints out the list of job titles you will read through them and pick out the jobs you would be interested in learning more about. If you're ready, let's start.

Frame 1

AOEIS will help you select job names (occupations) through the choices you enter. Please enter a number from the following list. The numbers and their areas are:

1. Interests	5. Working Conditions
2. Areas of Work	6. Education
3. Physical Strengths	7. Temperaments
4. Physical Capabilities	

Please enter one number from the list above (1, 2, 3, 4, 5, 6, 7)

C: I'd like to start with number 1, interests.

Frame 2

Which of the following would you like to work with?

Data
People
Things

Press one of the following letters (D, P, T) then press return to continue.

C: Data and things . . . I don't know. I think people.

Frame 3

You have selected 173 AOEIS titles. You have used area number 1.

1. Interests   5. Working Conditions
2. Areas of Work   6. Education
3. Physical Strengths 7. Temperaments
4. Physical Capabilities

Do you wish to select another area? Please enter No or the next area number (2, 3, 4, 5, 6, 7)

C: Maybe look at kinds of work next, press #2.

Frame 4

Which of the following kinds of work would you like to do?

Business and Clerical   Personal and Protective Services
Humanities and Human Relations Science, Mathematics and Engineering
Medical and Related Services   Trades and Industry

Press one of the following letters (B, H, M, P, S, T)

C: I guess Business and Clerical.

Frame 5

You had 173 AOEIS titles and now have 63. You have used area numbers 1, 2

    1. Interests   5. Working Conditions
    2. Areas of Work   6. Education
    3. Physical Strengths   7. Temperaments
    4. Physical Capabilities

Do you wish to select another area? Please enter No or the next area number (3, 4, 5, 6, 7)

C: Physical strength, I'll look at that next.

Frame 6

What kind of physical work do you want to do?

    Light work — lifting less than 20 pounds
    Medium work — carrying things weighing up to 50 pounds
    Heavy work — carrying things weighing more than 50 pounds

Press one of the following letters (L, M, H) and press return to continue

---

C: I'm strong, but I don't like to lift heavy things. I'll choose light.

Frame 7

You had 63 AOEIS titles and now have 62. You have used area numbers 1, 2, 3

    1. Interests   5. Working Conditions
    2. Areas of Work   6. Education
    3. Physical Strengths   7. Temperaments
    4. Physical Capabilities

Do you wish to select another area? Please enter No or the next area number (4, 5, 6, 7)

C: Let's do physical capabilities.

Frame 8

> If you *do not want* to do one or more of the following:
>
> $\underline{C}$limb and balance
> $\underline{H}$andle, reach, finger, and feel
> $\underline{K}$neel, stoop, and crouch
> $\underline{S}$ee
> $\underline{T}$alk and hear
>
> Press the letters of the choices you *do not* want to do and then press return to continue.

C: I don't want necessarily to talk and hear.

Frame 9

> You had 62 AOEIS titles and now have 42. You have used area numbers 1, 2, 3, 4
>
> 1. $\underline{I}$nterests   5. $\underline{W}$orking Conditions
> 2. $\underline{A}$reas of Work   6. $\underline{E}$ducation
> 3. $\underline{P}$hysical Strengths   7. $\underline{T}$emperaments
> 4. $\underline{P}$hysical Capabilities
>
> Do you wish to select another area? Please enter No or the next area number (5, 6, 7)

C: Let's try working conditions.

Frame 10

> At your job, where would you like to work?
>
> $\underline{I}$ndoor work place
> $\underline{O}$utdoor work place
> $\underline{B}$oth inside and outside everyday
>
> Press the letter that matches your choice (I, O, B)

C: I don't like summer in Arkansas, so I want indoor work.

Frame 11

You had 42 AOEIS titles and now have 40. You have used area numbers 1, 2, 3, 4, 5

    1. Interests   5. Working Conditions
    2. Areas of Work   6. Education
    3. Physical Strengths   7. Temperaments
    4. Physical Capabilities

Do you wish to select another area? Please enter No or the next area number (6, 7)

C: I think I'll go through all areas so I'll choose education next.

Frame 12

Pick how much school or training you want before getting a job (you may pick more than one)

    1. No high school diploma   6. Community college
    2. On-the-job training   7. Apprenticeship
    3. High school diploma or GED   8. Bachelor's degree
    4. Vocational school diploma   9. Master's degree
    5. Proprietary/vocational school   0. Doctorate (Ph.D. or Ed.D.)

Press the numbers that match your pick (1, 2, 3, 4, 5, 6, 7, 8, 9, 0) then press return to continue

---

C: I don't like school that much but I could probably handle 2 years at a community college. I'll enter both high school diploma and community college.

Frame 13

You had 40 AOEIS titles and now have 27. You have used area numbers 1, 2, 3, 4, 5, 6

    1. Interests   5. Working Conditions
    2. Areas of Work   6. Education
    3. Physical Strengths   7. Temperaments
    4. Physical Capabilities

Do you wish to select another area? Please enter No or the next area number (7)

C: OK, temperaments.

Frame 14

At your job, what kinds of temperaments would you like included? (You may pick more than one)

Accuracy	Logic
Creativity	Persuasion
Directing	Repetition
Evaluation	Stress
Interaction	Variety

Press the letters that match your choices (A, C, D, E, I, L, P, R, S, V) and then press return to continue

---

C: I'd like a job where I could be creative, interact with other people, use logic, and have variety.

Frame 15

You have selected 8 AOEIS titles. Do you wish to:

1. See a list of your AOEIS titles (occupations)
2. Change your choices and see a new list
3. Stop

Please enter 1, 2, or 3

C: Sure, I want to see a list of job titles.

Frame 16

The following AOEIS titles match your AOEIS profile

AOEIS Titles	Fiche
31 Bank Teller	DPT49
35 Building Manager	DPT14
53 Office Manager	DPT21
80 Food Service Manager	DPT18
101 Teacher Aide	DPT25
173 Medical Record Personnel	DPT53
370 Legal Assistant	DP20

It should be noted that it is not necessary to include all seven routes in the search to develop the profile; the more routes explored, the narrower the lists of job titles generated. The Searcher can stop at any point during the search process to view the list of job titles generated to that point. In addition, for job titles that do not appear on the list, the Searcher has the option of calling up those titles via the computer access codes. The program will list the search choices necessary to match these jobs and compare them to the choices made by the Searcher. These comparisons may be used to highlight issues for consideration during vocational counseling. For example, suppose an individual selected a two-year community college degree from the Education route. If this happened, the desired occupation of elementary school teacher would not appear on the occupational printout. The Searcher would have to rethink the decision regarding the amount of training he or she is willing to obtain or eliminate the occupation from consideration. Naive job seekers find this function very useful in that it delineates general job requirements that may not have been considered previously. Searchers are free to revise their choices until they are satisfied that the profile is an accurate reflection of their vocational preferences. Once satisfied, the evaluator typically covers the following information:

- Now that you are finished picking out the jobs, you will use another machine called a "microfiche reader." I have information about jobs on film called microfiche. (Demonstrate slipping the fiche in & the information flashing up onto a screen.)
- The microfiche will show you information about the jobs you're interested in learning about.
- Some of the information on the microfiche includes where to find the job, how much money you could make, your job responsibilities, and training required.
- You do not have to read all of the information. Just read what you are interested in learning.
- You can read about as many jobs as you want.
- Do you have any questions?

The evaluator and searcher would then look through the available microfiche files to learn more about specific jobs that were identified in the search.

FUTURE DIRECTIONS

The role of the microcomputer in rehabilitation has been established and will continue to increase in the future. The relative ease with which the information can be updated and the computer's "ability" to process large amounts of information makes it a powerful asset in the rehabilitation process. This project completed initial modifications and additions to make this technology available to hearing-impaired persons. Similar modifications are needed for other CIDS packages across the United States so that all interested hearing-impaired persons can access these improvements locally. Further refinement of this tool should serve to increase the ability of hearing-impaired job seekers to access timely and relevant career information.

REFERENCES

Arkansas Occupational and Educational System, (1982). Little Rock, AR: Arkansas Employment Security Division, Research and Analysis Section.

Austin, G. (Ed.). (1974), *Careers for deaf people.* Washington, DC: U.S. Department of Health, Education and Welfare.

Bullis, M. (1985). Vocational decision-making: A career education. In M. Bullis & D. Watson (Eds.), *Career education of hearing-impaired students: A review.* Little Rock, AR: Arkansas Rehabilitation Research and Training Center on Deafness and Hearing Impairment.

Bullis, M., & Watson, D. (1985). *Career education of hearing-impaired students: A review.* Little Rock, AR: Arkansas Rehabilitation Research and Training Center on Deafness and Hearing Impairment.

Dunn, W.L. (1982). *Status of statewide career information delivery systems.* Washington, DC: National Occupational Information Coordinating Committee.

Fitch, B. (1976). Career development in elementary and secondary education. *Gallaudet Today,* Summer.

Furth, H.G. (1973). *Deafness and learning: A psychosocial approach.* Belmont, CA: Wadsworth Publishing Co. Inc.

Gentile, A. (1972). *Academic achievement test results of a national testing program for hearing-impaired students, United States: Spring, 1971,* (Serial D, No. 9) Washington, DC: Annual Survey of Hearing-Impaired Children and Youth, Office of Demographic Studies, Gallaudet College.

McCray, P.M. and Blackmore, T.F. (1985). *National directory of rehabilitation facilities using computers.* University of Wisconsin Stout, WI: Research and Training Center Stout Vocational Rehabilitation Institute.

Moores, D.F. (1982). *Educating the deaf: Psychology, Principles, and Practices* (2nd ed). Boston, Houghton Mifflin.

National Occupational Coordinating Committee (1982, July). *The status of the NOICC/SOICC network: September 30, 1981.* NOICC Administrative Report No. 6.

Passmore, D. (1983) in D. Watson, G. Anderson, N. Ford, P. Marut & S. Ouellette (Eds.), *Job placement of hearing-impaired persons: Research and practices.* Little Rock, AR: Arkansas Rehabilitation Research and Training Center on Deafness and Hearing Impairment.

Schein, J.D. (Ed.) (1977). Current priorities in deafness. *The Volta Review.*

Watson, D. (Ed.), (1976). *Deaf evaluation and adjustment feasibility.* Silver Spring, MD: National Association of the Deaf.

Watson, D., Anderson, G., Marut, P., Ouellette, S., & Ford, N. (Eds.) (1983). *Vocational evaluation of hearing-impaired persons: Research and practice.* Little Rock, AR: Arkansas Rehabilitation Research and Training Center on Deafness and Hearing Impairment.

CHAPTER 6

JOB-SEEKING SKILLS TRAINING WITH DEAF REHABILITATION CLIENTS

NANCY M. LONG

THE CHIEF objective of any rehabilitation plan is that of "optimal vocational adjustment" (Bolton, 1976; p. xvii). For most clients involved in the rehabilitation process, this translates into successfully obtaining and maintaining employment. To reach this goal, rehabilitation counselors concern themselves with provision of services that will assist clients to (1) prepare for a job; (2) find a job; and (3) ultimately keep the job (Vandergoot, Jacobsen, & Worrall, 1979). Of these three service areas, the topic of "job placement" (i.e., finding a job) has been the focus of numerous discussions and articles outlining the priorities of rehabilitation counselors. Rubin and Roessler (1978) argued that once all pre-employment goals have been met, rapid placement of clients in suitable jobs is the primary concern of rehabilitation counselors. For deafness rehabilitation counselors, the activities in the job placement process become even more salient, as they are often the chief resource for assisting deaf persons to find employment (Amrine & Bullis, 1985). These responsibilities become even more critical if one considers the increase in numbers of unemployed deaf persons (Christiansen, 1982) and the extremely limited amount of time that rehabilitation counselors actually invest in client placement activity (Zadny & James, 1979). As a result, many agencies are encouraging their clients to develop more self-reliant means by which to enter the job market.

For deaf clients, implementation of this approach is not without complexities. As described by Amrine and Bullis (1985), the task of securing a job can be "frustrating, demoralizing, and seemingly a futile effort" (p. 1). For the deaf person, job-seeking problems are often compounded by difficulties in communication, a poor understanding of the job-seeking process, and negative employer attitudes towards hiring a disabled person (Schroedel & Jacobsen, 1978). Indeed, in order to address these issues, deafness rehabilitation practitioners interested in job placement would need to devise a way to assist their clients to overcome many of the difficulties they will encounter, and to do so in a way that is both time and cost efficient. This approach would provide overworked and often overwrought deafness rehabilitation specialists with innovative methods for increasing effective client placement. At the same time it would serve to decrease client reliance on the counselor for "repeat performances" of job placement activities in the event of subsequent termination(s) of employment.

In addressing the placement issues faced by many deafness rehabilitation counselors, attention has turned to the development of systematic programs for teaching self-directed job placement skills for job-ready clients (Dwyer, 1983; Long & Davis, 1986; Torretti, 1983; Torretti & Hendrick, 1986). The basis for these approaches is that people should be taught the skills needed to find employment on their own (Wesolowski, 1981). Benefits of this approach include increased investment by the **client** in securing and maintaining employment as well as allowing the rehabilitation counselor to work more effectively with a larger number of clients.

Most formal self-directed job-seeking skills training (JSST) programs are derived from the landmark work of Azrin and Besalel (1980) in their publication, **Job Club Counselor's Manual: A Behavioral Approach to Vocational Counseling.** Utilizing a highly-structured approach, the "Job Club" teaches persons not only the successful techniques for securing employment, but does so by conveying the message that job seeking is a full-time endeavor. The philosophy underpinning the "Job Club" approach to JSST is that intensive behavioral (skills) training will result in clients learning the skills that will make them successful at securing employment (Amrine & Bullis, 1985).

Relying heavily on the behavioral techniques of modeling, shaping, rehearsal, role-play and positive reinforcement, members of a "Job Club" group learn the appropriate actions and responses needed to successfully compete with other job applicants. "Job Club" groups provide each participant with opportunities to learn and practice skills while also experiencing the benefits of group support. The "Job Club" approach has been demonstrated to be an effective strategy with the chronically unemployed (Azrin & Philip, 1979), persons with physical disabilities (Kauss & Soto, 1981), blind persons (Dickson & Macdonnell, 1982) and psychiatric rehabilitation clients (Jacobs, Kardashian, Kreinbring, Ponder, & Simpson, 1984).

This chapter is one result of a cooperative agreement between University of Arkansas Rehabilitation Research and Training Center on Deafness and Hearing Impairment (RT-31) and the Tulsa Speech and Hearing Association/Projects With Industry Program (TSHA/PWI). Through this relationship, research data were collected to evaluate the effectiveness of a JSST approach in improving clients' abilities to secure employment. JSST implementation guidelines presented are the result of the experience of the TSHA/PWI in teaching job-seeking skills to clients who were enrolled in that program from February through December, 1984. Demographic information collected on clients who participated in the training during this time period revealed that the "typical" participant was a severely to profoundly deaf young adult of approximately 30 years of age. This "typical" client was a male who had been unemployed for at least the year prior to entering the TSHA/PWI, was prelingually deafened, and relied primarily on sign language for purposes of communication.

JOB-SEEKING SKILLS TRAINING: OVERVIEW OF THE MODEL

Program Techniques

Drawing on the original "Job Club" model, the TSHA/PWI JSST teaching methods included didactic instruction, positive reinforcement, shaping, and direct client involvement in the job search. Similar to the Azrin and Besalel model (1980), responsibilities were assigned for counselors as well as clients involved in self-directed JSST. In general, the counselor's responsibility in this approach is to provide an environment which facilitates client learning of necessary skills to obtain employment. Specific counselor duties include:

- scheduling and holding JSST sessions
- providing appropriate and correct demonstrations of desired behaviors

- providing feedback to shape clients' responses
- providing feedback to increase clients' pride and self-esteem
- assisting with location of job leads
- monitoring client progress and providing extra assistance as needed for skill acquisition
- encouraging positive interaction between clients and fostering a cooperative group atmosphere

Similarly, clients must have their own responsibilities which are discussed and agreed to within the context of a contract. Client duties include:

- regular and full attendance
- full and maximum effort
- adherence to the contractural agreement

Working in small groups, it was the responsibility of the TSHA/PWI program JSST counselor to provide direction, opportunities for practice, and feedback to the clients. Clients in the group were assisted in providing each other with support, encouragement, and motivation. Through this process of combining the efforts of counselors and clients, the goal of client employment was frequently reached. In order to facilitate this outcome, it was particularly important that a contractural agreement be reached between the program (counselor) and the client. This agreement served to delineate the duties, responsibilities, and expectations of both parties (i.e., the program and the client). In the case of deaf clients, this formal written agreement, negotiated by both parties and signed by the client and counselor, often served as a visual cue for the client to refer to in later discussions. It also served as a means by which to familiarize, i.e., emphasize, the importance of completing group activities designed to assist members in meeting each other and forging a "common bond." The Job Placement counselor met with each client individually to discuss employment interests, experiences, and aspirations, as well as to describe more fully the JSST program with its expectations and responsibilities.

The remainder of this chapter will address specific suggestions for implementation of a JSST program with hearing-impaired clients. References to particular issues that arose with TSHA/PWI clients will be made when appropriate to the topic.

The first step in any skills training program is that of assessment. This holds for JSST activities as well. This "Job Club"/JSST approach being described here first assessed clients on their level of knowledge of information pertaining to job seeking and job maintenance. Clients who performed particularly well on the pretest could be excused from attending parts of the formal training and only be required to engage in selected JSST activities.

Consistency and frequency of meetings are critical issues in the successful implementation of any JSST program. "Job Club" originators recommend a full-time approach (i.e., 40+ hours per week); many deafness rehabilitation professionals have cited other programming considerations that often conflict with this recommendation such as vocational training, independent living skills training, etc. The TSHA/PWI groups met formally, 4 days per week for one month for training purposes. Mornings were divided evenly with two classes each week devoted to the JSST and the remaining two meetings focused on related work adjustment training. Afternoon meetings were less structured with clients engaging in job-seeking skills practice, role-plays and other related job-seeking activities. These 20 afternoon meetings allowed clients to put to use the information or skills learned in the formal meetings.

Program Topics

Seven topics that comprise the basic components of job seeking were included in the program. Each of these topics and special tips regarding their implementation are described in subsequent sections.

Developing a Resume. Material discussed in this area was focused on the content included and the format to be used in preparing a resume. Deaf clients typically experience some difficulty in understanding the concept of reverse chronological order when listing work experiences. Special effort should be taken in explaining this concept. Difficulty may also be experienced by clients when attempting to identify the skills required of them on previous jobs. Again, special effort should be made to have clients identify and list any and all of their job responsibilities and requirements from previous employment positions. This may require the counselor to engage in role-play or pantomime situations where clients demonstrate their previous job tasks.

An important issue related to resume development with this population concerns disclosure of the client's hearing impairment. There seems to be two schools of thought on this issue:

1. Deaf applicants **should not** inform employers of their impairment prior to the employment interview. This approach provides the deaf person the opportunity to discuss his/her hearing impairment

in person and by example to demonstrate one's capabilities rather than disabilities related to the hearing impairment.

2. Deaf applicants **should indicate** on their resumes that they have a severe hearing impairment. Typically, this is accomplished by putting a statement in the identifying data section of the resume that acknowledges the hearing impairment while stressing that the impairment does not render the client incapable of performing well on the job. A typical example of this statement is as follows:

Health: Excellent. I do have a severe hearing impairment but this does not affect my ability to work.

The rationale behind this approach is that it may allow an employer advance time to become familiar with utilization of interpreters or other communication strategies if the employer so desires.

Resolution of this issue is best accomplished on an individual basis for each client. A discussion of the advantages and disadvantages of both options should allow clients to make an informed decision and to state their preferences.

Job Leads. Job leads, for any job seeker, can be found in several places. The newspaper want ads are an obvious starting place, as are public and private employment service agencies. Friends and family often provide valuable job leads. The clever job seeker may find valuable information in news media coverage of new plants opening, or through the expansion of local businesses. Valuable job lead possibilities can be found in the yellow pages of local telephone directories. The job seeker with specific skills could find the names of local businesses that specialize in the same type of skill, and then contact those places to inquire about employment. These job lead sources are applicable to and often utilized by deaf persons with some modifications.

One major souce of job leads involves use of newspaper **want ads.** However, the wording and abbreviations seen in newspaper want ads are often confusing even to the most fluent English speaker, and for a person to whom English is not necessarily a first language, they may seem undecipherable! The clients of the TSHA/PWI benefitted greatly from classroom discussion (with supplemental handout vocabulary lists) of the abbreviations seen in the want ads (see Fig. 6-1 for example). Use of these lists greatly reduced the complexity and often prevented future difficulties experienced by clients who could refer to their own lists when necessary.

HELP WANTED

SEC-Word Proc. to $14K

(deal with Clients-Business Exec.
daily; gd skills/personality)
General Office; Type 40; 10 Key;
phones; Data Entry $4.50
Credit clerk Trainee-good typist;
office exp; benefits . . . . $695 Raises
RECEPTIONIST typ 45, pho .$800 Up
Legal Sec-displaywrtr . . . .$$
Legal Sec-Word Process . . . . . . .to $13K
SEC 20up prefer Word Proc. $12K
DATA Entry-prefer Medical $900
Gen. Ofc v. Lt typ-phon . . . .$600 +

Sample Vocabulary List

Exec.	= Executive; boss
gd	= good
Typ 40	= type skill 40 words a minute
10 key	= skill at 10 key adding machine
exp	= experience; other jobs like this
sec	= secretary
12K	= Thousand dollars; earn $12,000 year
phon	= phone; must use telephone
clk	= clerk

Figure 6-1. Sample want ad.

Although **employment service agencies** offer a viable strategy for obtaining job leads, many deaf persons encounter difficulties in utilizing these agencies. The primary reason for these difficulties stems from the typical lack of prior experience with hearing-impaired persons exhibited by employees at these agencies. The recommended approach for solving this problem is twofold: placement specialists should invest time in providing "deaf awareness training" to employees of these agencies as a group and individually; and encourage clients to use assertive behavior and appropriate use of interpreters to prepare for these difficult situations.

Friends and family members are probably the most viable and frequently utilized source of job lead information for the deaf individual. Clients should be encouraged to take advantage of these sources in addition to all other possible sources of job leads. However, special attention should be paid to the independence of the client. Clients should be encouraged to actively control as much of the job-seeking process as possible since the more effort invested by the client, the greater the likelihood of a successful placement. Where possible, family members and friends should be discouraged from acting as interpreters or placement specialists in this effort.

The **news media** proves to be a somewhat limited source of job lead information for the deaf client since the ability to read and understand newspaper news/articles becomes an issue. Efforts to overcome this obstacle on a formal basis can include regularly scheduled time for the clients and counselor to discuss local news events of relevance.

Successful utilization of **telephone directory yellow pages** in obtaining employment requires knowledge of generalizable work skills, the ability to use a directory, as well as the ability to make "cold calls" to employers to ask about employment opportunities. These skills were not readily demonstrated by most clients of the TSHA/PWI. Remediation of these deficits requires intensive training and practice, particularly with regard to appropriate use of interpreters in placing telephone calls to employers. Clients should be encouraged, when making telephone calls with the assistance of an interpreter, to introduce themselves as "hearing-impaired" or "deaf" and to indicate that they are communicating by use of an interpreter. This often alleviates the difficulty that arises when John Doe, a deaf man, introduces himself over the phone in the female voice of an interpreter. In addition, clients benefit from being coached on presenting an explanation on the role of the interpreter, including the fact that there will be time lags involved.

Making Initial Contact. Clients often require assistance in composing letters of introduction to go along with resumes. In general, guidance should be provided on the general categories of information to be included in such a letter, e.g., request for interview or meeting, a way to contact the client, an explanation of his/her assets, skills, and experience and how these might be used to the benefit of the company. Clients in the TSHA/PWI worked well when given some flexibility in the ordering of this information. Counselors often provided feedback or the "fine tuning" of English grammar sentence structure. Typing services for the letters of introduction and resumes were provided by the TSHA/PWI support staff.

Setting Up the Interview. Setting-up interviews with employers can be approached in conjunction with the topic of making initial contacts. Clients benefit from role-play situations designed to improve their skills in these areas. Group interaction and positive, constructive feedback can be strongly utilized as part of the role-playing experience. An added dimension to these topics involves not only the appropriate use of an interpreter, but also the responsibility of the client to arrange for an interpreter to be available. This responsibility is particularly important during the stage of setting-up an interview. Clients who must share interpreting services might be allocated certain interpreting "time slots" in which to schedule interviews. If the client wishes to use the same interpreter for telephone calls and interviews, the two should agree beforehand on dates and times when the interpreter can be present for the client interview. Again, appropriate utilization of interpreters requires not only interactional skills on the part of the client, but organizational skills. Unfortunately, with some clients of the TSHA/PWI, learning the lesson of scheduling interpreter services was accomplished "the hard way" with missed appointments and frustrated clients, counselors, and employers. However, with practice, encouragement, and positive feedback, most were able to master, to the best of their ability, the skills required.

Completing Applications. A great deal of time should be devoted to working with clients on the topic of completing job applications. Clients may not understand what information is being requested due to ambiguous language or use of abbreviations. Attention may be given to vocabulary building and synonym structuring, i.e., asking for the same information using different wording. For example, application forms vary in the way educational information is asked for. "Education," "Highest Degree Completed," "Highest Grade Attended," "Highest Grade Completed," and "Educational Attainment" are but a few of the ways clients may be requested to list their educational level.

It is strongly recommended that several different sample application forms be obtained for use in practice by the client. The importance of answering all questions should be stressed, possibly with "guest lectures" from local employers addressing the negative effect that blank spaces on an application form have in considering a job applicant.

The Interview. Training, practice, and the behavioral concept of "shaping to appropriate response" are the key words for addressing this topic of the JSST. In didactic form, clients may be given information on the importance of "giving a good interview" for employment success. The critical elements of a good interview that are introduced and described include: appropriate dress, appropriate manners, eye contact, presenting information on relevant skills, experiences and education, and ending the interview on a positive note. This information is put into practice with videotaped (if possible) role-play experiences for evaluation and feedback. Clients are assisted in mastering the skills needed in the interview to introduce and use an interpreter, and ask for clarification if an employer's question is not understood. Clients seem to benefit from the role-play experiences as they serve to aid in gaining mastery and self-confidence. If possible, it is recommended that local employers, perhaps from agency advisory board sources, be utilized in the interviews. The inclusion of "real employers" lends credibility to the role-play for the client, and more closely approximates what the clients will encounter in interviewing for employment.

Follow-Up. The importance of clients contacting employers after they have been interviewed should be stressed. Clients may do so in a letter or via telephone. Form letters may be preferred due to the convenience of copying the body of the letter and later typing in different employer names and addresses as needed. The messages to be conveyed in a follow-up contact include: appreciation for the interview, continued interest in employment with the particular company, and availability for a second interview or to answer additional questions.

GUIDELINES FOR IMPLEMENTATION

Setting

As previously mentioned, a JSST program for hearing-impaired persons should offer information in a consistent and frequent manner. This translates into an intensive program that requires clients to meet regularly; daily group meetings are highly recommended. For agencies that offer additional service programs, the TSHA/PWI model offers a viable option for meeting this recommendation. Their system of formal training meetings, two mornings per week, with afternoon time devoted to practicing and utilizing job-seeking skills proved successful with the population served.

Client Characteristics

Group composition may vary in accordance with communication modes and the size of the staff available to work on this program. Groups of extremely mixed communication modes are difficult to deal with effectively; clients and counselors both suffer. Extreme variability may be acceptable if there are several staff members assigned to the JSST program who might serve as interpreters, assistants, etc. Some practitioners recommend that all group members be equated for their "level of experience as a job seeker." In other words, first-time job seekers would be put together in one group. Unfortunately, logistical considerations frequently dictate that most groups are formed as a result of time and opportunity. It was the experience of the TSHA/PWI staff that clients presenting varying levels of job seeking skills often provide opportunities for peer modeling and reinforcement. This, in combination with "individualized" afternoon activities, seemed to outweigh any disadvantages that might arise in conjunction with differences in skill acquisition.

Service Provider Characteristics

Group leaders should possess fluency in most, if not all, communication modes utilized by deaf persons. The optimal group leader should also possess strong counseling skills and a background in vocational rehabilitation. The group leader(s) should be thoroughly familiar with the training program that is utilized and, above all, should possess maximum flexibility for adapting any and all facets of the training program to meet the needs of any particular client or group.

SUMMARY AND FUTURE DIRECTIONS

Any "Job Club" technique, and any client graduate of a "Job Club" program will find the successful utilization of skills highly dependent on extraneous factors. No matter how skilled clients may become at job interviewing, if there are limited job opportunities or negative employer attitudes, clients may be thwarted from demonstrating their skills. It is recommended that an agency or facility that considers implementing a "Job Club" program simultaneously implement, or increase, employer development activities.

Throughout its existence, the TSHA/PWI program has experienced a high placement rate. Approximately 65 percent to 70 percent of the clients who had participated in the training were able to secure employment within a relatively short time. It should be pointed out however, that the JSST program of the TSHA/PWI, is one of the three components which operate to improve the employment of deaf persons. It would be difficult, if not unfair, to claim that the JSST program was solely responsible for the placement success reported. The employer development and other support activities (e.g., interpreter services) undertaken by TSHA and the TSHA/PWI did much to improve the attitudes and receptiveness of employers to the idea of hiring deaf/hearing-impaired persons. A program which offers a balance of both client-oriented **and** employer-oriented activities seems most likely to be successful and is recommended as the optimal approach.

REFERENCES

Amrine, C., & Bullis, M. (1985). The Job Club approach to job placement: A viable tool? *Journal of Rehabilitation of the Deaf, 19*(1-2), 18-23.

Azrin, N.H., & Besalel, V.A. (1980). *Job Club counselor's manual: A behavioral approach to vocational counseling.* Baltimore, MD: University Park Press.

Azrin, N.H., & Philip, R.A. (1979). The Job Club method for the job handicapped: A comparative outcome study. *Rehabilitation Counseling Bulletin, 23*(2), 144-155.

Bolton, B. (Ed.). (1976). *Handbook of measurement and evaluation in rehabilitation.* Baltimore: University Park Press.

Christiansen, J.B. (1982). The socioeconomic status of the deaf population: A review of the literature. In J.B. Christiansen & J. Egelston – Dodd (Eds.), *Socioeconomic status of the deaf population.* Washington, DC: Gallaudet College Press.

Dickson, M., & Macdonnell, P. (1982). Career club for blind job seekers. *Journal of Visual Impairment and Blindness, 76,* 1-4.

Dwyer, C. (1983). Job seeking and job retention skill training with hearing-impaired clients. In D. Watson, G. Anderson, N. Ford, P. Marut, & S. Ouellette (Eds.), *Job placement of hearing-impaired persons: Research and practice.* Little Rock, AR: University of Arkansas Rehabilitation Research and Training Center on Deafness and Hearing Impairment.

Jacobs, H.E., Kardashian, S., Kreinbring, R.K., Ponder, R., & Simpson, A.R. (1984). A skills-oriented model for facilitating employment among psychiatrically disabled persons. *Rehabilitation Counseling Bulletin,* 87-96.

Kauss, P., & Soto, M. (1981). Job club and transferable skills: Models for placement of severely handicapped. *American Rehabilitation, 6,* 7-11.

Long, N.M., & Davis, G. (1986). Self-directed job seeking skills training: Utilization in a projects with industry program for deaf persons. In D. Watson, G. Anderson, & M. Taff-Watson (Eds.), *Integrating human resources, technology, and systems in deafness.* Silver Spring, MD: American Deafness and Rehabilitation Association, Monograph No. 13.

Rubin, S.E., & Roessler, R.T. (1978). *Foundations of the vocational rehabilitation process.* Baltimore: University Park Press.

Schroedel, J., & Jacobsen, R.J. (1978). *Employer attitudes toward hiring persons with disabilities: A labor market research model.* Albertson, Long Island, NY: Human Resources Center.

Torretti, W.M. (1983). The placement process with severely disabled deaf clients. In D. Watson, G. Anderson, N. Ford, P. Marut, & S. Ouellette (Eds.), *Job placement of hearing-impaired persons: Research and practice.* Little Rock, AR: University of Arkansas Rehabilitation Research and Training Center on Deafness and Hearing Impairment.

Torretti, W.M., & Hendrick, P. (1986). A job club approach with severely disabled deaf clients. In D. Watson, G. Anderson, & M. Taff-Watson (Eds.), *Integrating human resources, technology, and systems in deafness.* Silver Spring, MD: American Deafness and Rehabilitation Association, Monograph No. 13.

Vandergoot, D., Jacobsen, R., & Worrall, J. (1979). New directions for placement practice. In D. Vandergoot & J. Worrall (Eds.), *Placement in rehabilitation: A career development perspective.* Baltimore: University Park Press.

Wesolowski, M.D. (1981). Self-directed job placement in rehabilitation: A comparative review. *Rehabilitation Counseling Bulletin, 25*(2), 80-89.

Zadny, J.J., & James, L.F. (1979). The problem with placement. *Rehabilitation Counseling, 22*(5), 439-442.

CHAPTER 7

SINGLE SUBJECT RESEARCH DESIGNS IN APPLIED PRACTICE: EVALUATING THE EFFECTS OF EMPLOYABILITY ENHANCEMENT INTERVENTIONS

STEVEN E. BOONE, MICHAEL BULLIS, and GLENN ANDERSON

THE CHAPTERS in this book have described a number of interventions and strategies that may be used to enhance the employability of deaf persons. Presumably, adopting these techniques will be of benefit to **our** clients. However, it is also important for us to assess the usefulness and efficacy of these interventions for our clients: to ensure that the strategies we use in our practice are producing or have produced the desired outcomes for our clients. Most of us agree with this goal. We want to be as effective as possible in assisting our clients and to have the sense of competence that develops from doing our best and seeing its outcome with clients. Unfortunately, it is difficult to subjectively determine if our methods are working in many instances. Rarely are changes dramatic, especially in the short run. More frequently, they occur slowly and in small steps. These changes are difficult to identify, unless we systematically collect information regarding our clients that will enable us to assess these changes.

While most of us agree with the goal of evaluating our practice and holding our methods accountable, we are hesitant to take the next step and collect data. This hesitancy may stem from a number of reasons including attitudinal factors (I'm a practitioner, **not** a researcher!), practical limitations (I don't have the time to collect data! Wait until the end of a study to serve "control group" clients? Impossible!), and knowledge or skill deficiencies (I want to evaluate my practice, but I don't know how!).

The purpose of this chapter is to introduce the reader to single subject research designs as a potentially valuable way to evaluate the effects of our interventions with clients. As compared to other fields, these designs are relatively underutilized by deafness rehabilitation professionals. Of the numerous studies published yearly in the field that relate to educational techniques, habilitation/rehabilitation methods and behavioral interventions, most have relied on group research methods. This chapter will present the rationale for single subject designs, describe more commonly used types of designs, and provide examples of their use in deafness. The chapter is intended as a brief introduction and overview; there are a number of in-depth books available for a more thorough review (Sidman, 1960; Hersen & Barlow, 1976; Chassan, 1979; Johnston & Pennypacker, 1981; Kazdin, 1982; Poling & Fuqua, 1986).

THE RATIONALE FOR SINGLE SUBJECT DESIGNS

Single subject designs (also called single organism, single case, or $N = 1$ research methods) refer to a group of techniques wherein one subject (or in some instances, a small group of subjects) is studied intensively with each subject serving as his or her own control. The heart of these methods is the repeated measurement of behavior over time. The general strategy is to measure the client's behavior (the dependent variable) to obtain a stable estimate of the level of behavior that is occurring prior to treatment (called the baseline) and then implement the intervention or treatment procedure (the independent variable). The level of behavior measured during baseline and treatment are compared to assess the effectiveness of the intervention. The generality of the findings is assessed by replication of the procedure over time and with other clients.

In order to use these designs, the practitioner/researcher must initially define the target behavior(s) as objectively and specifically as possible within its situational context (e.g., work setting, classroom, living situation). A focus is placed on the dimensions of behavior per se, its frequency, quality, timing, and form in different situations. In general, target behaviors may be considered as excesses (those behaviors that occur at too high a frequency or intensity for a situation) or deficits (those behaviors that occur at too low a frequency or intensity for a situation).

A wide variety of data collection procedures can be used including self-report, mechanical recording devices, or direct observations. For example, suppose the target is to improve a general problem that may have been traditionally labeled "poor work motivation." This problem could be operationalized more specifically in terms of on/off task behavior while the client is at work completing an assembly task. Assessment data obtained via a self-report method might ask the client to report the number of items assembled in a specified length of time. A mechanical recording device could also be used to count the number of items completed. Finally, observers could periodically sample the client's behavior, observe if he or she was assembling the product and record the results.

All single subject designs utilize an initial period of observation in which the level of target behavior is recorded. This initial period of measurement is described as "baseline" and is usually labeled as "A" on a graph of the design. Subsequent "treatment" phases of activity are also graphed and given labels (e.g., B, C). All graphs of data plot the level of behavior over time. Baseline and treatment phases are usually separated from each other using a dotted line.

FUNDAMENTAL DESIGNS

There are two fundamental categories of single subject research designs, each of which may be used to evaluate the effects of an intervention on a client's behavior or, more technically, to establish a functional relationship between an independent variable (a treatment program, intervention, or instructional procedure) and a dependent variable (the behavior that is targeted for change). These two categories of designs, withdrawal and multiple baseline, differ in the procedures used to assess change. The subsequent sections review the rationale and procedural aspects of each of these designs as well as their relative advantages and disadvantages.

Withdrawal Designs

A-B-A-B Design. The most common type of withdrawal designs is the A-B-A-B design. In this design, baseline is collected (A) and then the treatment (B) is instated. The treatment is withdrawn (A) and then reinstated (B). The effectiveness of the intervention (IV) is assessed and inferred from changes in behavior (DV) observed when the treatment is instated, withdrawn and then reinstated. A graph of a typical "effective" intervention is presented in Figure 7-1. As may be seen in the graph, upon introduction of the treatment, there was an observable change in the target behavior. Upon "withdrawal" of the treatment, the level of behavior reverted to its baseline levels.

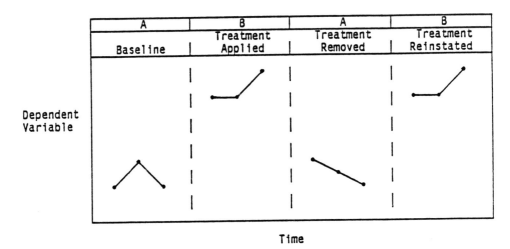

Figure 7-1. Illustration of the sequence of conditions in an A-B-A-B withdrawal design.

As an example of the use of this design, suppose a rehabilitation professional is interested in improving the cooperation of a multiply disabled deaf worker in a sheltered workshop while cleaning up. Cooperative behavior (the number of times the client offered to assist coworkers during clean-up activities) would be measured throughout a baseline period. The intervention (providing reinforcers for helping coworkers) would then be instituted and changes assessed. The treatment would be removed and subsequently reinstated. The intervention would be deemed effective if an increase in cooperative offers was found during periods of the intervention and a decrease in cooperative offers was found when the intervention was removed.

Advantages and Disadvantages. This "withdrawal" design represents a fairly straightforward method for assessing the effects of an intervention on behavior, allowing the practitioner/researcher to examine the functional relationship between treatment strategy and student/client behavior. This design controls for the effects of potential rival hypotheses such as history and maturation. Accordingly, if other extraneous variables not associated with the treatment strategy were responsible for the behavioral change, the behavior would not be expected to revert back to the baseline rates during the second "A" phase.

Thus, a key issue when considering the use of these types of designs is that the intervention must be one that can be easily removed and reinstated in a treatment or instructional program.

The disadvantages of using these types of designs are primarily associated with the withdrawal strategy. Use of the withdrawal strategy can be undesirable when for ethical or practical reasons it is not appropriate to allow the client's behavior to return to previously unsatisfactory levels. Also, because of the importance of repeated measurement, the more complex types of withdrawal designs can be time consuming and present potential logistical problems related to scheduling and adequacy of resources. Furthermore, in some applications it is difficult to utilize the withdrawal strategy if improvements in the client's behavior generalize and maintain over time. While it is obvious that this is the desired effect, it may be impossible to assess the effectiveness of the intervention in instances when upon removing the treatment, the client's behavior does not return to baseline levels.

Multiple Baseline Designs

Researchers and practitioners often encounter situations whereby it is either inappropriate to allow student/client behaviors to return to baseline levels or the effects of treatment intervention cannot be removed. In these instances, a multiple baseline design may be a viable alternative to assess the functional relationship between a treatment strategy and behavior change. The three major types of multiple baseline designs which do not rely on the withdrawal procedure to demonstrate change are discussed below.

Multiple Baseline Across Behaviors Design. In an across behaviors design, concurrent measures of **two or more target behaviors** exhibited by **one individual** are obtained over time to establish baselines against which changes can be evaluated. Implementation of this design requires that the target behaviors are independent from one another. After stabilization of baseline data, the intervention is applied to one of the target behaviors while baseline measures are continued on the other behaviors. The intent is to measure and assess change in the targeted behavior (dependent variable) while the other behaviors remain, hopefully, unaffected by the treatment intervention. This procedure is continued in sequence until the treatment intervention has been applied to all the target behaviors. A functional relationship between the treatment intervention and the dependent variables would thus be demonstrated if change occurs in the target behaviors **only** after treatment is applied, while the baseline rates for the untreated behaviors remain stable.

Figure 7-2 provides a graphic illustration of this type of design. Notice that the rate of two behaviors is plotted over time and the broken line represents the point at which the interventions were applied. As may be seen in the results, one would infer that a functional relationship exists between the intervention and the behavior. Upon introduction of the intervention on target behavior one, an increase in the desired behavior was found; no change occurred on target behavior two, until the intervention was introduced on this behavior.

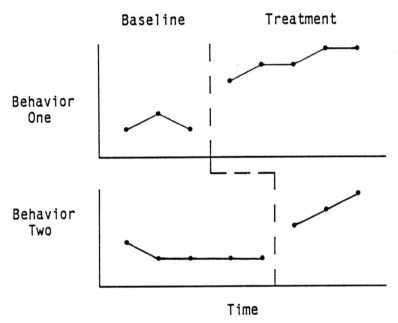

Figure 7-2. Illustration of the sequence of conditions in a multiple baseline across behavior design.

As an example of a multiple baseline across behaviors design, suppose a counselor is interested in assessing the effects of social skills training on the interpersonal communication skills of a deaf college student described as shy and unassertive. The target behaviors might be those associated with having a conversation with female students such as initiating the conversation (e.g., Hi, it's good to see you today.) and asking for a date (e.g., Would you like to go out for a pizza next Friday?). After baseline measures have been taken and stability achieved, the intervention would be applied sequentially across each of the target behaviors. The effectiveness of the intervention would be inferred if the target behavior increased following intervention and there was no change on the untreated target behavior.

Multiple Baseline Across Individuals. In an across individuals design, a treatment intervention is applied in sequence across two or more individuals with the same target behaviors. Thus, in contrast to the across behaviors design, an across individuals design focuses on a **single** targeted behavior **across two or more individuals.** This type of design (see Fig. 7-3) involves the sequential application of a treatment intervention to each individual, one at a time. Thus, a functional relationship between the treatment intervention and the dependent variable would be demonstrated if the individual intervened upon first shows a change in the target behavior while the behavior of the individual who had not had the intervention remains the same.

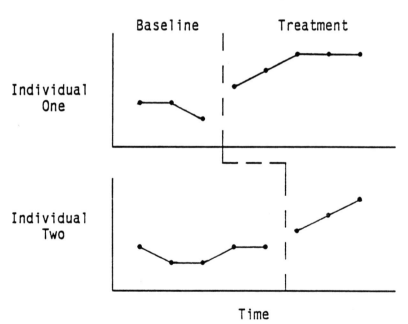

Figure 7-3. Illustration of the sequence of conditions in a multiple baseline across individuals design.

For example, a counselor might be interested in assessing the efficacy of a job-seeking skills training program on teaching two deaf rehabilitation clients how to complete job applications. The dependent measure could be the percent of applications that are completed appropriately. Baseline measures of the dependent variable would be taken on both clients at the same time. After stable baseline rates are achieved, the job-seeking skills training program would be given sequentially to the first client and the rate of appropriate completed applications would be assessed. The job-seeking skills training program would be considered effective if the number of applications correctly completed increased following training for the trained client and no increases were demonstrated found for the client who had not been trained.

Multiple Baseline Across Settings. In an across settings design, a treatment intervention is sequentially applied to the target behavior of a **single** individual across **two or more independent settings or situations.** A functional relationship between the treatment intervention and the dependent variable would be demonstrated if a change in the target behavior was observed only subsequent to intervention in the setting. For example an administrator of an interpreter training program might be interested in assessing the impact of a particular training curricula on reducing an interpreter's anxiety while interpreting in a variety of different situations. The dependent measure could be the number of times the interpreter asks a speaker to repeat what was said. The target situations could be interpreting lectures in a college classroom, interpreting telephone conversations, and interpreting staff meetings. The implementation of baseline measures and the treatment intervention would follow similar procedures and steps as those described for across behaviors and across individuals designs. Figure 7-4 graphically illustrates this type of design. As may be seen in the graph, a reduction in "requests for repetition" occurred only after the intervention was applied in each setting.

Advantages and Disadvantages. The major advantage of multiple baseline designs involves their usefulness in applications where it is either considered undesirable to allow target behavior to return to baseline levels or impossible to remove the effects of the treatment interventions. Practically, this may enhance obtaining support from service providers because interventions and services to students/clients do not have to be interrupted or withdrawn to demonstrate effects. Another advantage of multiple baseline designs is that by focusing on the measurement of several concurrent behaviors, the design allows for a closer approximation of naturalistic conditions since an individual tends to make a variety of responses at the same time to environmental stimuli (Hersen & Barlow, 1976).

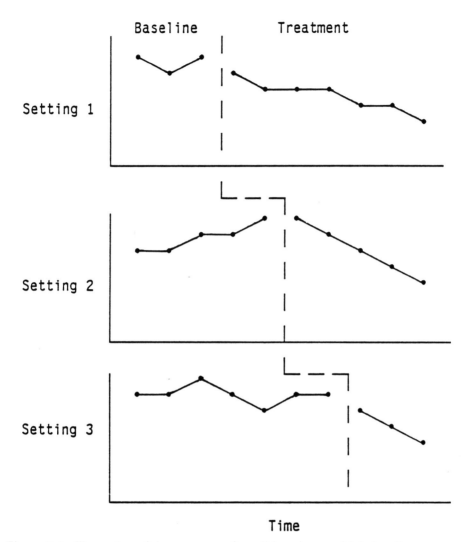

Figure 7-4. Illustration of the sequence of conditions in a multiple baseline across settings design.

A disadvantage of multiple baseline designs is that they provide a weaker demonstration of experimental control than withdrawal designs (Hersen & Barlow, 1976). Consequently, at times it becomes difficult for an investigator to readily determine if changes in the dependent variable are due to treatment per se, or if the effects are related to other extraneous variables.

Another disadvantage relates to the basic assumption that the dependent variables (i.e., the targeted behaviors, situations, or persons) are

independent from one another. For example, if the two target behaviors measured in an across behaviors design are related to each other, intervening on one behavior may also produce similar, but unexpected, changes on the second behavior. If this occurs, it is difficult to infer the controlling effects of treatment. Similar problems may arise in across situation designs (e.g., changes occur in both situations when intervention has only been applied in the first situation) or across persons designs (e.g., changes occur for both persons even though the intervention has only been applied to the first person).

A final point related to considering the use of multiple baseline designs is deciding on the number of baselines that are needed to demonstrate a functional relationship between treatment interventions and behavior change. In general, the more baselines across which the effect of an intervention is demonstrated, the more convincing is the demonstration of a possible functional relationship. In most cases, however, a minimum of three baselines is recommended (Kazdin, 1982, Hersen & Barlow, 1976).

ANALYSIS OF SINGLE SUBJECT DATA

For most purposes, data collected in single subject designs are analyzed visually through examination of graphs such as the ones provided. This practice is in part related to the notion of clinically versus statistically significant change. For example, in treating a worker who engages in disruptive and inappropriate behaviors in the work setting, one is not as concerned with a statistically significant decrease in these behaviors as much as with their absence or reduction to an acceptable level for that environment. In other words, the numerical analysis may achieve statistical significance but be meaningless in terms of actual behavior requirements of the setting. Visual interpretation of data allows for a more realistic assessment of clinically significant change.

In practice, one of the major factors in interpreting single subject data concerns the stability of baseline data prior to the introduction of the treatment. One collects data until a representative level of the behavior has been determined. Ideally a graph of this data would be perfectly stable (e.g., occurring at the same rate over time). Unfortunately, this is rarely the case, as a client's behavior may significantly fluctuate over time. In these instances, the practitioner/researcher must continue to collect data until a pattern is identified that can be used to compare the results of the intervention. Examples of patterns that may be appropriate are presented in Figure 7-5. In general, one's confidence in assessing the adequacy of a baseline is increased if there is good stability, little variability, and a large number of points in the baseline.

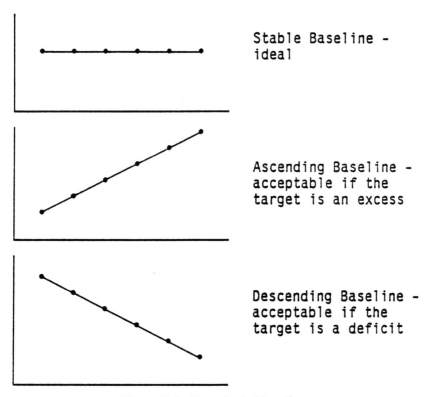

Figure 7-5. Hypothetical baselines.

Although there are no hard and fast rules on how to inspect and evaluate data, a number of considerations add to one's confidence in looking at changes and interpreting their significance (Martin & Pear, 1978). In general, results can be viewed more confidently if the finding has been replicated a number of times, if the treatment and measures are specified precisely, and if the results are consistent with accepted theory. Other criteria include if there are few overlapping data points between baseline and treatment conditions, if the change is large, and if the change occurs quickly following the introduction of treatment. For a more detailed discussion of the issues in the visual interpretations of data, refer to Paronson & Baer (1986).

In recent years, statistical analysis of single subject data has been proposed to detect subtle fluctuations in data sets that may be indicative of practical and clinical significance (Jones, Vaught, & Weinrott, 1977; Kazdin, 1976) and to reduce imprecision found in the visual analysis of a graphic display of data (DeProspero & Cohen, 1979; Ferlong & Wanipold, 1981). Subsequently, great debate has emerged on the importance of statistically analyzing single subject data and the appropriate method to utilize in such analysis (Baer, 1977; Michael, 1974, 1977). At present, it should be noted that the statistical analysis of single subject is controversial and that there are no hard and fast rules regarding the use and interpretation of the statistical analysis of single subject research data. For the reader who is interested in the particulars of the statistical analysis of single subject designs, the previously cited articles and an excellent chapter by Kazdin (1976) should be reviewed.

REFERENCES

Baer, D. (1977). Perhaps it would be better not to know everything. *Journal of Applied Behavior Analysis, 10,* 167-172.

Chassan, J.B. (1979). *Research design in clinical psychology and psychiatry, 2nd Ed.* New York: Irvington Publishers, Inc.

DeProspero, A., & Cohen, S. (1979). Inconsistent visual analysis of intrasubject data. *Journal of Applied Behavior Analysis, 12,* 573-579.

Furlong, M., & Wanipold, B. (1981). Visual analysis of single subject studies by school psychologists. *Psychology in the Schools, 18,* 80-86.

Hersen, M., & Barlow, D. (1976). *Single case experimental designs.* Elmsford, NY: Pergamon Press.

Johnston, J.M., & Pennypacker, H.S. (1981). *Strategies and tactics of human behavioral research.* New York: Erlbaum.

Jones, R., Vaught, R., & Weinrott, M. (1977). Time series analysis in operant research. *Journal of Applied Behavior Analysis, 10,* 151-166.

Kazdin, A. (1976). Statistical analysis for single-case experimental designs. In M. Hersen & D. Barlow (Eds.), *Single case experimental designs.* Elmsford, NY: Pergamon Press.

Kazdin, A.E. (1982). *Single-case research designs: Methods for clinical and applied settings.* New York: Oxford University Press.

Martin, G., & Pear, J. (1978). *Behavior modification: What it is and how to do it.* Englewood Cliffs, NJ: Prentice-Hall.

Michael, J. (1974). Statistical inference for individual organism research: Some reactions to a suggestion by Gentile, Roden, & Klein. *Journal of Applied Behavior Analysis, 7,* 627-628.

Michael, J. (1977). Statistical inference for individual organism research: Mixed blessing or cure: *Journal of Applied Behavior Analysis, 7,* 647-653.

Paronson, B.S., & Baer, D.M. (1986). The graphic analysis of data. In A. Poling & R.W. Fuqua (Eds.), *Research methods in applied behavior analysis: Issues and advances.* New York: Plenum.

Poling, A., & Fuqua, R.W. (1986). *Research methods in applied behavior analysis: Issues and advances.* New York: Plenum.

Sidman, M. (1960). *Tactics of scientific research.* New York: Basic Books.

CHAPTER 8

FUTURE DIRECTIONS

DOUGLAS WATSON and GLENN ANDERSON

A PRIMARY GOAL of vocational rehabilitation services in the 1980s is to prepare deaf individuals to "earn a living and live a life" (Rochlin, DeCaro, & Clarq, 1983). As such, this implies that rehabilitation services should be directed, for the most part, towards preparing deaf individuals to make transitions from school and/or training to work and community living. This goal further implies that in order to make successful transitions deaf individuals will need to acquire technical, personal, and social competencies to obtain, maintain, and advance in the workplace as well as function independently in the community. In spite of the advances made in the postsecondary training and rehabilitation of deaf people in the past 20 years, it has been noted in the professional literature that many deaf rehabilitation clients frequently experience problems making satisfactory adjustments in a variety of life domains — vocational, social, community living (Arkansas Rehabilitation Research and Training Center on Deafness, 1985). Neff (1977) cited two areas as most often needing attention. The first is concerned with clients' skills in the domain of vocational adjustment while the second focuses upon facilitating clients' personal and social functioning. Neff described both areas as employability enhancement skills.

In response to these needs this monograph presented several interventions designed to address the employability enhancement skills of deaf clients. These interventions were based on a three-stage employability enhancement model developed by the Arkansas Rehabilitation Research and Training Center on Deafness that emphasized Life and

Career Planning, Social and Job Preparation, and Employment Seeking. Targeted toward specific stages of this model, each of the interventions described in this monograph has demonstrated potential for
enhancing the life and career planning, social and job preparation, and
employment seeking potential of deaf rehabilitation clients. Within the
past few years, several programs and agencies throughout the U.S. have
begun to incorporate various components of the RT-31 employability
enhancement skills training model within their service delivery systems.
This is an encouraging trend and it is anticipated that employability
enhancement skills training will soon become a key component of rehabilitation programming for deaf clients.

In order for the field of deafness rehabilitation to maximize the potential of deaf individuals to "earn a living and live a life," it will need to
look beyond the individual client's problems and target potential support
groups within the client's environment. Support groups such as family
members, employers, and the individual's social network (hearing and
deaf) are presumed to play a significant role in enhancing a deaf client's
transition from school and/or training to work and community living.
For example, deaf rehabilitation clients may possess the technical, social, and interpersonal competencies necessary for successful employment, but be unable to demonstrate their skills and qualifications if they
encounter employer resistance due to negative attitudes and a lack of
knowledge about deafness (Arkansas Rehabilitation Research and
Training Center on Deafness, 1985).

Historically, the resources of environmental support groups such as
the family, employers, and social network have not been adequately
tapped to complement employability enhancement service delivery to
deaf clients. In part, this problem persists because of the lack of empiri-
cally validated interventions shown to encourage the contributions of
these support groups in the employability enhancement of deaf clients.
In response to these concerns, RT-31 will expand its research program
during the next five years (1986-1991) to address the development of interventions that focus not only on the individual client within the Center's three-stage model of employability enhancement, but also upon the
support groups within the deaf client's environment.

FUTURE DIRECTIONS

The Arkansas Rehabilitation Research and Training Center on
Deafness (RT-31) intends to expand its research program to address not

only the needs of individual clients, but also the support groups within the clients' environment. The mission of the Center is to conduct a program of research and training activities with the ultimate objective organized around the central theme of **Enhancing Rehabilitation Outcomes of Deaf Persons.** Specific efforts will be directed to enhance both vocational and psychosocial adjustment. Conceptually, this mission is schematically represented in Figure 8-1. Within each core area, Center

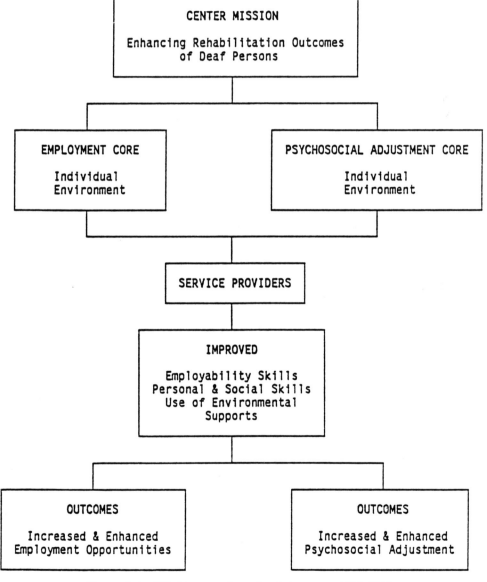

Figure 8-1. RT-31 research and training core: 1986-1991.

activities are focused on two sets of factors, individual clients and their environment. Individual client factors include the knowledge, skills, abilities, and attributes that the client brings to or develops through the rehabilitation process. Environmental factors include the specific sources of support that are available to clients either during the rehabilitation process or in their subsequent living or work setting.

Two programs of research and training will be developed within the central theme.

1. **Enhancement of Employment Outcomes of Deaf Persons.** This program addresses the development of interventions to enhance the transition of deaf persons from school to workplace and support services that contribute to their successful employment and career development. Research and training in this core area will address the continuum of employment development from career assessment and planning to follow-up support services that contribute to career establishment, maintenance and advancement.

2. **Enhancement of the Psychosocial Adjustment of Deaf Persons.** This program will address the development of interventions to enhance the communication, personal and social adjustment skills of deaf persons. Research and training in this core area will focus on the participation and utilization of family members and the larger deaf community as key support groups having an impact on the psychosocial adjustment and development of the deaf individual.

Both research and training core areas involve the use of a programmatic approach for the identification, development, demonstration, and dissemination of interventions to enhance employment and psychosocial adjustment. Each core area includes material development and training projects to enhance the dissemination and utilization of new techniques for the improvement of rehabilitation outcomes of deaf persons through the use of employment and psychosocial adjustment interventions. The two programs of research are directed at the ultimate goal of enhancing rehabilitation outcomes of deaf persons.

As previously mentioned, the first program addresses the development of interventions to enhance transition of deaf persons from school to the workplace. The literature shows that many deaf persons have been denied normal developmental experiences, resulting in deficits in their career planning, aspirations, and preparation. Entering the labor force with incomplete and erroneous information and expectations, many experience additional problems in establishing and maintaining themselves as they do not have the basic skills required to successfully adapt in work settings. The research in this program will address these problem areas by:

1. identification of the factors that influence and shape the career aspirations of deaf youth and adults;
2. identification of the factors that promote successful transitions from school to the work setting;
3. comparing the preceptions, motivations, and attitudes of employed and unemployed deaf workers toward work and rehabilitation;
4. development and demonstration of promising interventions for use in career information, exploration, and guidance;
5. development and demonstration of interventions with employers to assist deaf persons establish and maintain employment; and
6. dissemination and training strategies designed to promote use of the interventions by rehabilitation and other practitioners.

The second research program addresses the development of interventions to enhance the communication, personal and social adjustment skills of deaf persons. Because of the crucial importance of these respective skill areas to successful psychosocial adjustment, these research studies will focus upon the identification and development of:

1. technologies to assess independent living skills, problem solving abilities, and manual communication competencies;
2. measures to assess family involvement in the rehabilitation process;
3. strategies to assess the effects of the deaf community on the deaf individual's community adjustment;
4. interventions to plan rehabilitation programs;
5. interventions to increase participation and utilization of family members in the rehabilitation process;
6. techniques that make effective use of the deaf community as a support network; and
7. dissemination and training activities targeted to rehabilitation counselors, independent living specialists, mental health rehabilitation personnel, education staff, as well as parent and consumer groups.

SUMMARY

As previously noted, while the primary goal of vocational rehabilitation in the 1980s is to prepare deaf individuals to "earn a living and live a life," many deaf persons, compared to nondisabled persons, experience difficulties making suitable adjustments in the workplace and the community. These difficulties experienced by deaf individuals are attributed, in part, to their lack of skills in a variety of life domains (e.g., employment, social, and community) and in part because they lack effective support mechanisms in the work and community environments to make satisfactory transitions. There is a clear need for rehabilitation research concerned with enhancing the rehabilitation outcomes of deaf people as it relates to work and community living (e.g., vocational and psychosocial adjustment).

Accordingly, RT-31 is developing two programs of research to address these needs. The first focuses on enhancing employment outcomes and the second on enhancing psychosocial adjustment. Both programs will include systematic efforts to promote dissemination and utilization, as well as develop new assessment and intervention techniques that can be used by rehabilitation service providers.

If you are interested in obtaining more information or potentially being involved to field test developing interventions, please contact the Center.

Research and Training Center on Deafness
4601 W. Markham
Little Rock, AR 72205

REFERENCES

Arkansas Rehabilitation Research and Training Center on Deafness. (1985). *Application for funding of a rehabilitation research and training center for the deaf and hearing-impaired (G0086C3501)*. Washington, DC: National Institute on Disability and Rehabilitation Research.

Neff, W.S. (1977). *Work and human behavior* (2nd Edition). Chicago: Aldine Publishing Co.

Rochlin, J., DeCaro, J., & Clarcq, J. (1985). Competitive employment of disabled people: The need for a partnership. *Journal of Rehabilitation, 51*(2), 19-23.

INDEX